Samuel Rawson Gardiner

Documents Relating to the Proceedings against William Prynne

In 1634 and 1637

Samuel Rawson Gardiner

Documents Relating to the Proceedings against William Prynne
In 1634 and 1637

ISBN/EAN: 9783337047993

Printed in Europe, USA, Canada, Australia, Japan

Cover: Foto ©ninafisch / pixelio.de

More available books at **www.hansebooks.com**

DOCUMENTS

RELATING TO THE PROCEEDINGS AGAINST

WILLIAM PRYNNE,

IN 1634 AND 1637.

WITH A

BIOGRAPHICAL FRAGMENT BY THE LATE JOHN BRUCE.

EDITED BY

SAMUEL RAWSON GARDINER.

PRINTED FOR THE CAMDEN SOCIETY.

M.DCCC.LXXVII.

COUNCIL OF THE CAMDEN SOCIETY

FOR THE YEAR 1876-77.

President,

THE RIGHT HON. THE EARL OF VERULAM, F.R.G.S.

WILLIAM CHAPPELL, ESQ. F.S.A., *Treasurer.*
HENRY CHARLES COOTE, ESQ. F.S.A.
JAMES GAIRDNER, ESQ.
SAMUEL RAWSON GARDINER, ESQ., *Director.*
WILLIAM OXENHAM HEWLETT, ESQ.
ALFRED KINGSTON, ESQ., *Secretary.*
SIR JOHN MACLEAN, F.S.A.
FREDERIC OUVRY, ESQ. *Pres.* S.A.
THE RIGHT HON. THE EARL OF POWIS, LL.D.
JAMES ORCHARD PHILLIPPS, ESQ., F.R S. F.S.A.
EVELYN PHILIP SHIRLEY, ESQ. M.A.
REV. W. SPARROW SIMPSON, D.D. F.S.A.
JAMES SPEDDING, ESQ.
WILLIAM JOHN THOMS, ESQ. F.S.A.
J. R. DANIEL-TYSSEN, ESQ. F.S.A.

The COUNCIL of the CAMDEN SOCIETY desire it to be understood that they are not answerable for any opinions or observations that may appear in the Society's publications; the Editors of the several Works being alone responsible for the same.

BIOGRAPHICAL FRAGMENT

BY

THE LATE J. BRUCE.

It is not because WILLIAM PRYNNE stands in our literature as one of our most voluminous authors, nor because he is conspicuous in our history as a sufferer for conscience' sake, that I desire to interest the great body of English readers in his biography. His works, and the circumstances of his personal history, considered simply by themselves, deserve the attention of the scholar and the historian, but taken in connection with the general incidents of the times in which he lived they acquire a much higher importance and have a far more extensive application. Viewed in that relation, they enlarge our knowledge of the momentous transactions which occurred in England between 1625 and 1660; they give us views of men and events nearer and more distinct than can be derived from the wide survey of the general historian; and they enable us—which is more valuable than anything else—to drink deep into the general spirit of that eventful period. It is of the greatest importance that the history of that birth-time of our modern freedom and our consequent greatness should be thoroughly understood. I hope that the life of William Prynne, which I have endeavoured to write upon the principle I have indicated, will conduce in some slight degree to their being so.

CHAPTER I.

WILLIAM PRYNNE'S ANCESTORS.

The family from which William Prynne descended derived both its name and origin from the county of Salop. Looking down from Wenlock Ridge on the broad and fertile expanse which spreads for many miles towards the west, the eye is attracted at the distance of a few miles by several gentle eminences, just raised above the level of the surrounding country. These grassy knolls were anciently designated "Preens."[a] On one of them the Lords of Castle Holgood erected, in the old times, a house of religion devoted to the Cluniac monks—a cell to the magnificent Priory at Wenlock.[b] But all traces of this modest establishment[c] have long since disappeared. A "Great Preen" and a "Little Preen," the names of which may also be discovered in the records,[d] are not now to be found on the map. "Church Preen" remains alone to fix the locality and indicate the nature of these ancient pointed hillocks. From the time of Henry I. there dwelt on one of these Preens a family which

---

[a] The word *preon*, *prein*, or *preen*, signified originally "a point." Hence it was applied to a pin, and in that sense is still common in Scotland. The *fibula*, a brooch fastened by a pin, was designated by the same word, and its meaning was extended so as to comprehend a graving tool or other instrument terminating in a sharp point.

[b] Dugdale's Monast. v. 42. Tanner's Notitia Monast. Shropsh. 32.

[c] The priory of "Preone" is mentioned in Pope Nicholas's Taxation as possessed of two carucates of land, with a mill, a dove-cote, and other usual sources of the revenue of landed proprietors, producing altogether an annual income of £8 3s. 4d. Two cows and three pigs, which are also enumerated by the careful assessor, are valued at 6s. 9d. per annum. (*Tax. Eccles.* p. 164 b.)

[d] Rot. Hund. ii. 91.

was identified with its place of residence, either from ownership or long possession. These were the "De Preens," and afterwards, when the prefix "De" went into disuse, the Preens; but as a family they were historically undistinguished—no mention of them has been traced in any authentic annals. In an after-age some officer of the College of Arms found indications in the darkness of an indefinite period of an "Ambrose Pryn" of Kynveston in the county of Salop.[a] This Ambrose was in all probability a mere heraldic worthy, adopted upon slight evidence, or no evidence at all, by some Garter or Clarencieux at a time when officers of arms possessed a kind of instinctive facility in the recovery of the forgotten ancestors of *parvenû* families. From Ambrose was deduced a goodly progeny. Pryns with the Christian names of Andrew, Alexander, and Edward, followed in due succession for perhaps a couple of centuries, with a proper intermixture of Joans, and Isabels, and Marys. Thenceforward genealogical Pryns filled an ample page in the visitation books, and the shadowy demesnes of Kynveston, with other lands situate at a place conveniently described as "――――― in Worcestershire," continued for several generations to pass down, on paper, from father to son. In the sixth descent from the mythical Ambrose the reason for giving the Prynnes a genealogical respectability appears. This pedigree preparation ushers into notice two brothers, RICHARD and EDWARD PRYNNE, both flourishing merchants in Bristol—then the Liverpool of our ancestors. We now emerge into the light of day. Other informants more trustworthy than the early providers of pedigrees enable us for the first time to assign a date. Richard Prynne served Sheriff of Bristol in 1536 [b] and Edward Prynne in 1549.[c]

[a] Harl. MS. 1559, fo. 90; 1566, fo. 130; 1043, fo. 34.
[b] Barrett's Bristol, p. 684.
[c] Ibid. p. 685.

BIOGRAPHICAL FRAGMENT

From each of these Bristol magnates descended a race of **Prynnes**. Edward Prynne, **son of** Sheriff **Richard** Prynne, married "**a** daughter **of one of the** kingdom of Portugal,"[a] whose **fortune, or the capture of some** wealthy carrack, led to his knighthood. Dying without issue, **Sir** Edward's nephew Gilbert inherited his wealth. **Sir** Gilbert, for he also was afterwards knighted, resided at Allington, a hamlet of Chippenham, in the county **of** Wilts, and rests in the church of that town under a monument which indicates considerable wealth.[b] On Sir Gilbert's death without male issue his property was divided between his two daughters, and aided **their** accomplishments in procuring them admission into families **of the most dignified** descent. Seymour, the younger daughter, was married **to** Sir **George** Hastings, and carried her paternal arms into that shield **of** seventy quarterings which commemorated Sir George's descent from the Earls of Huntingdon and his many other connections with noble families.[c]

Frances, the elder daughter, was married to Sir Francis Seymour,[d] **afterwards** Baron Seymour of Trowbridge, a grandson of

[a] Harl. MS. **1559, fo. 90.**
[b] Beauties of England and Wales, Wilts., p. 526.
[c] Sir George was grandson of the puritan Earl Henry, and uncle of **Colonel Henry Hastings, the** cavalier commemorated by Clarendon (Rebell. book vi.) Sir George **died in July** 1641 of the plague, and was interred in the church of St. Bartholomew-**the-Great,** Smithfield. The coat of arms with the seventy quarterings was sus**pended** in his memory in that church. By his wife, Seymour Prynne, he had four **sons and three** daughters; but **his sons** all died without issue. Bell's Huntingdon **Peerage, p. 99.**
[d] **Sir Francis** Seymour was brother to the Earl of Hertford, who was governor to Charles II. **when** Prince **of Wales.** At the commencement of the reign of Charles I. **Sir** Francis was reckoned amongst the patriots (Strafforde Papers, i. 30); but he went over to the king **like** his friend Strafford, and was raised to the peerage **in** 1640. Egerton MS. 71, **is a** copy of a book of Meditations and Prayers written **by** him, and transcribed by **his** daughter Frances Viscountess Downe. **He** died **12 July,** 1664; his wife, Frances Prynne, died in child-birth in 1626. (Topographer **and** Genealogist, v. **31.**)

Katherine, sister to Lady Jane Grey, and great-grandson to the Protector Somerset. By these inter-marriages the great-granddaughters of the Bristol merchant—Richard Prynne—obtained niches in the pedigrees of many of our noblest families, and Frances, the elder, became distinguished as grandmother to the proud Duke of Somerset.

Whilst an ordinary succession of events was thus merging the descendants of one brother in families of the highest public distinction, the descendants of the other were pursuing a private but independent and not less reputable career. Edward Prynne had two sons, Erasmus and John. The latter sought fortune in London, and died there without issue. Erasmus is described as "of Clifton and Aust, in the county of Gloucester." The Clifton which stands to the west of Bristol had then no existence. The site of the streets and crescents which now rise majestically on that lofty eminence was in that day principally open pasture, and Erasmus Prynne, whose occupation was in connection with land, and his residence at Aust, which is a manor and hamlet in the parish of Henbury, had probably no other connection with Clifton than that he pastured his flock upon the wide expanse of Clifton and Durdham Downs. Erasmus Prynne had two sons, but our interest lies only with the second of them, whose name was Thomas. For some years he followed strictly in his father's steps; he tilled the land which had been in his father's occupation, and dwelt as his father had done in the old house at Aust. Towards the close of the sixteenth century Thomas Prynne, without altogether relinquishing his interest in Aust, removed to a better occupation. On the steep northern side of one of the narrow valleys which meet, as in a centre, at that most beautiful of English cities, Bath, and at the distance from the city of about two miles, stand the church and village of Swainswick.

The situation is singularly pleasant. In front, facing the west, across a narrow gorge, lies the village of Woolley, and above it rise the heights of Lansdown. Bath, with its abbey church, and its ranges of houses scaling the surrounding hill sides, are seen in the valley to the south, whilst beyond them the eye rests upon the verdant slopes of Prior Park. Northward, up the valley, lies the secluded Langridge. The cottages of Swainswick are scattered by the side of the narrow road which winds along the valley side, and which in the sixteenth century was a mule-track pursued by the chapmen who passed through the clothing districts of the West, and bore off, from house to house, the produce of the looms for sale. Since 1529 the cheerful sunny Swainswick has belonged principally to Oriel College, Oxford. The manor and the advowson of the church were in that year given to that college by one of their fellows, Dr. Richard Dudley, a clergyman of eminent station,[a] for the maintenance of two fellows and six exhibitioners. The place was almost entirely in the hands of Oriel College. They presented the rector, usually one of their fellows, and the chief layman in the parish was their "farmer," which in those days meant their agent, and the general manager of their property, as well as the tenant of their lands. A respectable residence, adjoining the churchyard on the north, was provided for this squire-farmer, and it was in this capacity that Thomas Prynne went to reside at Swainswick, between the year 1573[b] and the close of the century.

[a] Dr. Dudley had been master of St. Mary's Hall, and was afterwards chancellor of the cathedral of Salisbury. (Collinson's Somersetshire, i. 153; Wood's Hist. Antiq. of Oxford, ed. Gutch, Coll. and Halls, p. 671; Fasti, ed. Gutch, ii. 26, ed. Bliss.)

[b] In that year Edward Webb, "farmer," was buried on the 22nd June. (Swainswick Register, for access to which I am indebted to the kindness of the Rev. .) There was a monument to Webb in Swainswick church. (Collinson's Somersetshire, i. 155.)

In 1590, Bath was in a fervour of rejoicing at having obtained from Queen Elizabeth its first charter of actual incorporation. A glance at the map of the square little city as it then existed is sufficient to show the importance of this event. Approached on every side by roads long celebrated for being impassable in winter time, consisting of houses closely packed together in narrow streets, surrounded by a wall, and situate at the bottom of a heated basin in which water bubbles up of the temperature of [106°], it is easy to see how peculiarly necessary for the inhabitants must have been the power of self-government. The privilege had been obtained by the perseverance of a resident in the place, William Sherston, who had represented the city in parliament in 1583, and did so in the next four parliaments. His election for that service was no doubt an honourable distinction, but Sherston is most emphatically remembered by his fellow citizens as having been their first mayor after the charter. Sherston rented the home farm of the recently dissolved priory, and occupied its barton or farmhouse, the situation of which is indicated by the present Barton Street. The old farmhouse itself was long remembered as being the first house in Bath which was graced with the presence of the new regalia. Tradition has even asserted that it was honoured with more than the symbols of royalty, for that Elizabeth herself once slept under the roof of Mr. Sherston. Whether Thomas Prynne was present at the rejoicings which were sure to take place amongst our warm-hearted ancestors on such occasions, we cannot tell, but in mentioning this Barton house we approach as near as possible to the living farmer of Swainswick. It was a house with which he was intimately acquainted, in which his footstep must have been familiar, and the sound of his voice well known, for in that house he found a wife. He had been previously married, but was left a widower and childless. Marie Sherston, a daughter of the first mayor and the M.P., was willing to share with him the seclusion of Swainswick. When they were married does not appear, but in 1600 she gave birth to her second child but first son, WILLIAM PRYNNE, whose life I have undertaken to relate.

CHAPTER II.

WILLIAM PRYNNE'S HOME AND EDUCATION.

The home of William Prynne was one well suited for the nourishment of an earnest, serious spirit. That his father was a religious man is unquestionable. It is equally certain, from the explicit avowal of his theological opinions contained in the preface to his will, that, in the disputes of those days, he took the Puritan, or, as some people term it, the Calvinistic side. Such a man would be careful to teach his children and household to worship God in the way which he deemed right.

In worldly circumstances the Prynnes were in a position of comfort. Their residence, although an ancient fabric, and in its arrangements simpler than was quite in accordance with the growing luxury of the times, was comfortable and sufficiently spacious. The spot in which it was situate was cheerful and yet secluded; the surrounding country inspiring a sense of freedom from the considerable portion of it which was uninclosed, and yet negativing remoteness by its patches of cultivation, its pleasant gardens, and its neighbourhood to a considerable city. The peep, which is all that we are able to obtain, into the internal arrangements of this Puritan homestead pictures to us a roomy though not large abode. Amongst sitting rooms we find mention of the "parlour" and of Thomas

Prynne's "study," and amongst the sleeping rooms, besides that of the master, there are "the chamber" and "the little chamber" (two bed-chambers for guests), the "maidens' chamber," and "the chamber over the buttery," all furnished with chests and coffers, described from their several woods as of cypress, Spanish, or spruce, and complete with feather-beds, arras coverlets, sheets home-made and white as the driven snow, with many other substantial indications of domestic comfort. Neither were the requirements of good cheer nor the duties of hospitality neglected. There were "wine bowls" of several kinds, those of "white silver" being distinguished from "the best"; there was the "best salt," and "the silver gilt salt," and "the little silver salt" for every day, and the grand "piece of white plate" kept on the sideboard in a box, and a dozen "apostle spoons," and the silver spoons "with the square head," and there were "table boards" and "cup boards," and a profusion of platters, porringers, saucers, crocks, brass pans, and all the other means and appliances of a generous domestic economy. Here were evidently the external characteristics of one of those much-loved homes which are peculiar to the people of the middle class; homes rendered cheerful by industry and happy by general sympathy; homes equally removed from poverty and superabundance; the interests in which extend from the inmates to the surrounding neighbourhood, to which such homes are refuges in time of trouble, because in them the wants of the poor can be understood, and relief does not assume the form of condescension. The dwellers in the homes of what is termed "high life" may become acquainted with the wants and feelings of the poor, but they can do so only by study, as they may learn a language or a science; those in the middle class grow up into such knowledge from childhood.

Thomas Prynne's family increased around him slowly. Joan,

who was probably his eldest child, was born before 1600; William was born, as we have seen, in that year. Swainswick has always been said to have been his birth-place, but there is no register of his baptism, nor of that of his sister Joan, in that parish. Thomas followed in 1604; Katherine in 1607; Dorothy in 1610; and Bridget in 1613. These were all Thomas Prynne's children.

William Prynne derived his christian name from his grandfather, the Bath clothier, Sherston; and it seems likely that Sherston's residence was a frequent shelter to his godchild. William Prynne's first education away from home was received at the Grammar School in Bath. The distance was full two miles, and we cannot doubt that in the winter season the Barton house afforded him a frequent shelter.

Of his career at school I have not been able to recover any trace. I have not even found the name of his master. The school was one of Edward the Sixth's foundations, and in later times sent forth Sir Sydney Smith the admiral, and the Rev. Daniel Lysons the antiquary, and one of Prynne's successors as Keeper of the Tower Records. No one acquainted with Prynne's writings can doubt that he had in his youth a good foundation of solid learning.

The life of every man receives its primary colour from the scenes and companionship of early youth. That of Prynne was influenced by the opinions of his father, by the puritan books in the study at Swainswick, and by the public incidents in which his grandfather had a share. The earliest circumstance Prynne could remember was probably the Gunpowder Treason. His grandfather was one of the representatives of Bath in the Parliament which the conspirators doomed to destruction. As a child he was a witness to the demonstrations of affection with which his family and friends crowded round his grandfather on his return home after such an escape. Often in after-days may he have listened to the old man's narrative of the minute incidents of that enormous crime, **not** without occasional references to that greater national incident which must have been full in Mr. Sherston's remembrance, the defeat **of** the Armada. The revision of the translation of the Bible **was** another event which interested the family at Swainswick.

The first edition of our authorised version was published in 1611, and the variations between it and the favourite Geneva translation formed subjects of favourite speculation in puritan households. It was in the midst of these curious inquiries that the nation was suddenly plunged into the deepest grief by the death of Prince Henry. Some of us can remember the agony of national sorrow occasioned by the death of the Princess Charlotte of Wales. That sorrow stands in the recollection of those who shared in it as the only exhibition of national mourning they ever witnessed which deserves to have applied to it the terms general, sincere, profound. If historical testimony may be believed, it had its parallel on the occasion of the death of the heir apparent of King James I. The lamentation on that occasion was "so general," remarks Sir Simonds Dewes, with some want of gallantry, "as even women and children partook of it"; [a] and Sir Edmund Verney, after the lapse of seven and twenty years, refers to Prince Henry's death as the incident which up to that time had occasioned him the deepest grief.[b] In that part of the community to which Prynne and his family belonged, this loss was felt on more than general grounds. The calamities **which** ultimately resulted from the defects in the character of the sovereign had not yet produced their worst results. Carr, not Villiers, was the royal favourite; the Earl of Salisbury, who died only a few months before the prince, had hitherto restrained the king's extravagance; the Countess of Essex had not yet been divorced

[a] Autobiography, i. 46.
[b] Verney Papers, p. 210.

nor Overbury murdered ; but James had already proclaimed himself the determined enemy of all concession to puritanical scruples. At the same time that he threatened to "harry" the puritans out of the land, he gave encouragement to the stealthy advances of a formal semi-romish party in the church at home, and was full of undignified anxiety to cultivate friendly relations with the great Roman Catholic powers of France and Spain—especially the latter. In Prince Henry the nation lost a bulwark against Rome and the puritans an avowed protector. His death transferred the position of heir-apparent to a prince whose bodily infirmities had hitherto rendered necessary for him a life of seclusion ;—a reserved lad, of whose temper and character nothing was known.

From the Bath Grammar School Prynne passed, in 1616, as a commoner to Oriel College, Oxford. We may accept this fact as an indication that he had distinguished himself at school. The Swainswick farmer would scarcely have thought of sending his son to a university, and much less to the royal foundation, with which he himself may be said to have been connected, unless the boy had shown some aptitude for scholarship; probably, also, unless, on the ground of such aptitude, he had been encouraged so to do by those persons in authority in the college with whom he was brought into communication.

Prynne went to Oxford, a well-grown and intelligent youth, at a most important period. It was at the very time when the dissensions in the church of England were beginning to assume that form which ultimately led to its overthrow. In the reign of Edward VI. the new and apparently feeble Church of the Reformation naturally drew towards those foreign churches which had preceded England in separation from Rome. A common brotherhood was aimed at ; and although on some of the more recondite theological subjects there existed differences, such as must arise amongst bodies claiming independence of one another, it was desired on both sides to cultivate a general feeling of good will. Some of the great foreign theological scholars were received into England with favour, several of them were appointed to highly honourable offices in the church, and others were on various occasions consulted by our reformers with the greatest respect. On the accession of Elizabeth, this feeling was strengthened by the return of the Marian exiles and the increased popular aversion from Rome. The former had everywhere been treated kindly by the foreign churches, the latter was the inevitable result of the reign of Mary. Throughout the greater part of England pastors and laity were now forward in getting rid of everything which savoured of Rome. Altars were destroyed; fonts were removed; crucifixes, statues, images and pictures of the Deity or of saints were thrown down with iconoclastic zeal; the people felt no scruple in accepting the ministration of clergymen ordained by the hands of the presbytery in churches in which the order of bishops no longer existed; they were pleased to see the officiating ministers lay aside their copes and surplices and other apparel used in the old ceremonial worship; bowing at the name of Jesus, standing up at the *Gloria Patri*, and other old traditional usages, fell into disuse. Many of these alterations proceeded from the general inclination of ministers and people rather than from any mandate of authority. They were consequently not uniformly carried out. The queen herself was partial to a stately and dignified ceremonial. In many places the example of the royal chapel was accepted in the stead of a law; but there were whole counties and districts which went as far as possible the other way, and considered that in doing so they were carrying out the principle of the Reformation, restoring public worship to its ancient purity, and casting off the badges of Rome.

If this state of things had been permitted to continue throughout the reign of Elizabeth, it seems probable that at its close the ceremonial worship of the Church of England, the dress of the ministers and the mode of administering the sacraments, would **have been** nearly assimilated to those of the foreign protestant churches. But the queen was offended at the want of external uniformity. She insisted upon the bishops enforcing the surplice and the corner cap. They did so—some of them even against their own opinion—but it was at the expense of a schism. Retrogression even in things non-essential was by many persons deemed to be betrayal. The re-assumption of priestly costume was considered to be the first step towards reunion with Rome, and, therefore, was to be withstood at whatever cost. Thenceforward, the Church of England was split into two parties: a party which accepted no authority for either doctrine or practice save the revealed word of God, and aimed at a greater assimilation of the public worship to the simplicity, or as it was termed the purity, of primitive times—whence they were called Puritans; and another party which, being satisfied with the doctrine professed in the Church of England, was willing to take the will of the chief magistrate as their rule in all minor matters. On both sides there was considerable violence. The insolence of Martin Marprelate saved episcopacy; whilst the harshness with which a mere external uniformity was enforced by the bishops rendered the episcopal order unpopular, and threw into the puritan scale the good wishes, and when it was needed the active support, of all friends of liberty.

At the accession of James I. the majority of the nation were partially conforming puritans. They acquiesced in episcopacy as an ancient mode of church government, but disliked the pomp with which the bishops were surrounded and the worldly power with which they were endowed; attaching little importance to any religious forms, and especially disliking some of **those which were** retained in the church, as being inconsistent with the spirit of protestantism, they evaded or neglected **not a few** of the rubrical injunctions of the Prayer Book. In doctrine they upheld **the** calvinistic teaching of the Articles. Such were the opinions of the great body of the puritans. But there were amongst them, as in every party, and especially in every party of progress, ardent spirits who pushed all their opinions to what they esteemed their legitimate results. Such men submitted to bishops, but strove to prepare the public mind for the establishment of what they esteemed a more scriptural form of church government—that by a presbytery. In matters of form they desired closer assimilation to the foreign churches. In doctrine they openly contended for those logical deductions from election and predestination which the framers of the Articles left rather to be inferred than positively asserted.

Before his accession to the throne of England James **I. had been** for years struggling to revive a modified episcopacy in Scotland. He was therefore in no humour to relinquish **it in** England. Archbishop Bancroft was a great stickler for uniformity. The king aided him. The Elizabethan crusade in favour of surplices and corner caps was vigorously resumed. The puritans were everywhere depressed, and for a time it seemed as if great advance was made towards a uniformity in those external observances which as between the two parties within the church seemed too trifling to be worthy of dispute. Still the ministry and the universities were filled with men whose leaning was towards puritanism. Oxford is **said** to have been at this time like "a colony from Geneva."

But now arose in the church a new party, which not merely united with Archbishop Bancroft in insisting upon external uniformity, but sought to drive back the tide of Reformation to the very verge of Rome. By this party the name of protestant was repudiated, Diocesan Episcopacy was upheld as being of divine right, and the only channel through which men could become partakers of God's covenanted mercies; all the ceremonial **observances** of the pre-reformation church which could be fitted on, **so to speak**, upon the liturgy of the Church **of** England, were anxiously revised; the sacrament, now named the Holy Eucharist, was contended for as a real sacrifice; the officiating minister was consequently a priest; the sacramental elements acquired a **new** and mysterious character under his hand; and the apostolical succession was contended for as the only medium through which the true priestly authority could be derived. For some time these opinions made their way slowly and almost silently. A premature attempt to diffuse them at Cambridge failed, **and** the leader, after a reconciliation **in the Church of** England, found a more congenial refuge in the Church **of Rome.** Soon after the accession of James I. a more competent leader presented himself in the other university. William Laud, a fellow of **St. John's College, Oxford,** a man just rising into the prime of life, of irreproachable life, of unquestionable learning, and of daring courage—a man also of that refined subtilty of intellect which leads its possessors to delight in minute distinctions often imperceptible to ordinary inquirers—such was the person who thus stood forward. His first public avowal of these doctrines **took** place in 1604, when, at the age of 31, he maintained in the face of the university, on taking his degree of Bachelor of Divinity, that there could be no true church without diocesan bishops. **On** subsequent occasions **he broached** other opinions equally distinctive. His sermons pro**claimed open** war against the puritans, and indeed against all persons who were not willing to adopt a system, which, by its opponents, was considered to comprehend almost everything of popery save the pope: presbyterianism he pronounced to be "worse than popery." The avowal of such opinions raised an instant and violent outcry. The ardent divine was remonstrated with by his friends, and preached against from the university pulpit; he was even shunned in the streets as an obvious Romanist. But Laud was not a man who could be put down, nor did he stand alone. He had patrons who filled high stations, and were influential, both in church and state. Amongst them, his most zealous friend was Dr. Richard Neile, clerk of the closet to James I., and remembered for a piece of flattery which gave occasion to an excellent repartee from Bishop Andrewes. He has also another claim upon our recollection, in having passed through more bishoprics by translation than any other man who ever lived. Concurring in his opinions, Neile took Laud as his chaplain, and appointed him successively to livings in his dioceses of Rochester, and Coventry, and Lichfield, and ultimately introduced him to the king. His rise at court was delayed by the warning of Archbishop Abbot, and the active opposition of Lord Chancellor Ellesmere. Both these men were intimately acquainted with Oxford. They knew Laud and the character of his theology thoroughly. They concurred in opinion that his patronage by the king would turn to the detriment of the church, and they were able for several years to delay his advancement. The disheartened champion of anglo-catholicism would have quitted the court in despair but for the encouragement of his constant patron, Bishop Neile. Laud had preached his first sermon before King James on the 17th September, 1609. His friends anticipated immediate promotion. But it was not until seven years afterwards, until Lord Ellesmere's declining health had partially removed him from active life, that his patron, Neile, was able at last to procure for him the poor deanery of Gloucester. In the meantime, after a violent contest, he had succeeded to the mastership of his college. These eminent positions were turned with Laud's characteristic energy to the promotion of his theological party. To discourage and defeat puritanism was with him a matter of conscience. It was the business of his life, and no opportunity of doing so was ever lost. At Oxford, he kept the university in continual disturbance, by picking quarrels with public lecturers and authors, and with all other persons upon whom he could affix the brand of puritanism; and at Gloucester he instantly, in his new capacity of dean, affronted that great scholar Dr. Miles Smith,[a] the bishop of the diocese, by removing the communion table out of its then accustomed place, the body of the choir, placing it altar-wise against the wall at the east end of the choir, and introducing the practice of bowing towards it on entering the choir and also on approaching the table.

It was at this time that Prynne went to Oxford. The university rang with disputes, but the heads and tutors were little inclined to patronise Laud's Arminian or Popish novelties, as they were deemed by his adversaries, and the books used in tuition were all of the old puritan or Calvinistic stamp. Laud saw that without an alteration in this latter particular it was in vain to hope for that change in the opinions of the clergy which he desired to effect. He struck at once at the root of what he deemed the evil. He procured an order from the king for the better government of the university, by which the study of the Fathers, councils, and schoolmen was substituted for that of the abridgments and systems of theology founded principally upon the Holy Scriptures which were then in use. The whole course of theological study was thus to be revolutionised. All who dissented from Laud's divinity viewed the measure with fatal forebodings. In their estimation it poisoned the very fountains

---

[a] Dr. Miles Smith was celebrated for a wonderful knowledge of Hebrew and many other eastern languages. He and Bishop Bilson were the ultimate revisers of the authorised version of the Bible, and Dr. Smith wrote the preface to it. He never entered his cathedral after Dr. Laud's removal of the table and introduction of the practice of bowing towards it. (Wood's Athenæ, ed. Bliss, ii. 389; Heyling's Life of Laud, pp. 63, 64.)

of religious knowledge. The mazes of patristic theology could lead only to Rome.

Prynne was one of the students who came under the operation of the new mandate, but it may be doubted whether, in his time, it was fully carried out. The Vice-Chancellor, Dr. Goodwin, who was also Dean of Christchurch, together with Drs. Prideaux and Benefield, the professors of divinity, were all opposed to the change. Whatever partial obedience was yielded to it at first was merely out of respect to a document which proceeded from the king. Its promulgation whilst Prynne was at Oxford was probably the first thing which made him acquainted with the character and designs of the man between whom and himself there was thereafter to be the deadliest enmity. There is no evidence that Laud and Prynne met personally for several years after this time, but this interference with education concentrated upon Laud the puritan antipathies of the young scholar. Henceforth he watched the movements of the rising churchman with pre-determined hostility, and whilst Laud was scaling height after height in his ambitious course, fearing no man, and dreaming that every step he gained added to his security as well as his power, Prynne was feeding his antipathy with the observation of those acts of an anti-puritan and anti-protestant character to the accomplishment of which Laud's activity was ever prompting him.

The acquaintance which we find in Prynne's writings with the early literature of the church is probably in part to be attributed to this device of Laud. To stimulate him to a new course of study was its only effect upon Prynne. Faithful to the teaching and traditions of his home, and unscathed by all the bewilderments of tradition, he remained as firm a protestant and as much a puritan as ever.

Of the state of **Oriel** College whilst **he was** a student **we** can say little that is good. When he entered **the** college it was under the provostship of Dr. Anthony Blencowe, **whose** long headship **of forty-five** years was just drawing to a close. **On** the death of Dr. Blencowe, **there arose a contest for** the provostship between a son **of** the celebrated printer Day—Dr. John **Day, one** of the most eminent preachers of his time—and the **Rev. William** Lewis, whose chief qualification was his birth in **Merionethshire.** At **the** election, Day was defeated by **a** stratagem **of the Welsh fellows of** the college. A long litigation ensued. Day appealed **to** the **Bishop of** Lincoln as visitor ; his adversary sought the favour of the archbishop. **The** dispute was **then** taken before the lord chancellor, by whom **it was** referred to the attorney **and** solicitor general, **who** confirmed the **election of Lewis.** But **his triumph was** brief. Not being " able," **in the words of** the Oxford antiquary, " to conceal his amours," to **which "amours"** Prynne, **who** was in the college all the time, applies a highly offensive designation—so great an outcry was raised against him that he abruptly left the college and went abroad. In **1621, a few** months **after Prynne** left the college, Provost **Lewis** resigned.[a]

Wood speaks of Giles Widdowes, **a** fellow **of** Oriel **and afterwards** rector of Saint Martin's, Oxford, whom he describes **as a** harmless **honest man, but** " **of** so **odd** and strange parts **that few** or none could **be compared** with him," **as** having been Prynne's tutor.[b] That is

---

[a] The Rev. John Tolson, **the next** master, proceeded immediately after his election to pull down a part of the old buildings of the college and lay out a legacy left by Dr. Blencowe for erecting the south and west side of the present fabric. **The** remainder of the present college **was** erected in 1637, mainly **by** the exertions **of Dr. Tolson.**

[b] Athenæ, Bliss's ed., iii. **179, 844.**

a mistake. Prynne subsequently mentions this clerical Merry Andrew, with whom after a little while we shall meet again, in terms which are clearly incompatible with such relationship.[a]

Prynne took his degree of bachelor of arts on the 22nd January, 1620-1;[b] and left Oxford immediately afterwards.

CHAPTER III.

Prynne's choice of a profession.

During Prynne's residence at Oxford many changes had occurred in his home at Swainswick. Little Dorothy, his youngest sister, died at the age of six, during his first year at Oriel. His eldest sister Joan had been married to William Kemish, described as of Wickwar, in the county of Gloucester. The circumstances or position of her husband does not appear, but it would seem that he and his wife resided for many years at Swainswick. In January, 1617-18, they had a daughter born, who was named Katherine, and in September, 1619, a son named Arthur. But the event which exercised the greatest influence on the life of Prynne was the death of his father, which occurred on the 5th July, 1620. In compliance with his own directions he was buried in the parish church on the 10th July, and an inscription which at one time commemorated the place of his interment has now disappeared. By his will, which was made on the 1st February, 1618-19, he left his lease of his farm at Swainswick to his son William, charged with the payment of 200*l.* to his brother Thomas, and the same sum to each of his sisters,

[a] Prynne's book, *Lame Giles, his haltings*, was directed against him. S. R. G.
[b] Wood's Fasti, i. 392.

Katherine and Bridget. He left to William also a considerable portion of his furniture and plate, with some few articles to his other children, including Joan Kemish, who had no doubt received her portion on her marriage. He added, as an affectionate remembrance of her little daughter Katherine, a legacy to her of "two ewes and two lambs." There are also slight remembrances to his two grand-children Goffe. His will does not contain any provision for his wife, but she is mentioned in terms which negative any unkindness, and must therefore be presumed to have been otherwise provided for. Of his age or the circumstances of his death nothing is known. The ages of his children negative anything like extreme old age. Some persons might perhaps discover a presumption in favour of his sudden death in the circumstance that old Mr. Sherston, as if accepting the death of his son-in-law as a warning to himself, made his will within a few days after Thomas Prynne's interment—as soon afterwards in fact as in ordinary circumstances a will of such length could be prepared.

It is difficult to form an estimate of the value of the property which fell to the share of William Prynne on the death of his father. The only criterion seems to be found in the circumstance that Thomas Prynne expected that the legacies he had left, together with an allowance of twenty pounds per annum to his son William, might all be paid within five years. This would make the clear profits of his farm to amount to 150*l*. or perhaps 200*l*. per annum. Such an income was at that time a competent maintenance, and the question was no doubt mooted by the young Oxford bachelor of arts whether he should settle down at Swainswick and occupy his father's place. His father had given him the option of doing so by leaving him all the farming implements, but the lessons of an university ill accord with a life of rural retirement and inferior station. What may have been the determining motive which led him to the law rather than to the church, for which his subsequent writings prove him to have been well fitted, does not appear. In either profession a man of his laborious industry, determined purpose, and fearless courage, must have been pretty certain of success. He was admitted a student of Lincoln's Inn in the same year, 1621, in which he took his degree at Oxford; probably immediately afterwards.

During the reign of Elizabeth, Gray's Inn, the Inn of the Cecils and the Bacons, attained a certain pre-eminence in public consideration. Under James I. Lincoln's Inn, of old time the Inn of More and then that of Lord Ellesmere, was in the ascendant. The old mud walls, which separated Lincoln's Inn from Chancery Lane on the one side and "The Fields" on the other, disappeared in the reign of Elizabeth. About the time of the accession of James I. there arose a spirit of improvement in that part of London. The inhabitants of the City began to push out in a north-westerly direction beyond Temple Bar, and the talent of Inigo Jones was exerted in the erection of palace-like residences in the fields on the western side of Lincoln's Inn. The Inn partook in the general desire for improvement. An old gallery on the side of Chancery Lane was replaced by the existing buildings, and the services of Inigo Jones were called in aid to rebuild their old ruinous chapel. The present building, which is the one Inigo Jones designed, had been three years in the course of erection and was rapidly rising towards completion when Prynne entered the Inn.

It was only within the last forty years that Lincoln's Inn had engaged the constant services of a separate clergyman. Stirred up by the example of their brethren in the other Inns of Court, the benchers of Lincoln's Inn determined in 1581 to have a preacher of their own, and we may form an opinion respecting the religious opinions of a body of highly intellectual and intelligent Englishmen of that day by observing who were the persons to whom they applied to fill the vacant function. They first endeavoured to secure the services of Dr. Laurence Chaderton, master of the eminently protestant Emmanuel College, Cambridge, the college newly founded by Sir Walter Mildmay. Dr. Chaderton was afterwards one of the managers for the puritans at the Hampton Court Conference. Failing with him, they solicited Dr. John Reynolds, Regius Professor of Divinity at Oxford, and afterwards the other principal manager for the puritans at the same conference. Reynolds declined. They then appointed the Reverend William Clarke, a fellow of Peter House, but expelled the university for notorious puritanism. Clarke was succeeded at Lincoln's Inn by Field, one of the pillars of protestant theology—the Field of whom it was said that his memory smelleth like a field which the Lord hath blessed—the author of the celebrated book upon the church. Field was succeeded by the learned Gataker; a man of singular piety united to its proper concomitant of a large and liberal mind. For some years he was a member of the Assembly of Divines at Westminster. After the intervention of Dr. Holloway for four years, Donne the poet, who was already a member of the Inn, was appointed in 1616. He held the office at the time of Prynne's admission; some of his most eloquent sermons were preached in Lincoln's Inn Chapel; he had urged the Inn to the erection of the new fabric;[a] his hands had laid the first stone; and he was looking forward to the speedy completion of the work when the king removed him from his preachership by appointing him to the deanship of St. Paul's. The Inn

[a] " I, who, by your favours was no stranger to the beginning of the work, and an often refresher of it to your memories, and a poor assistant in laying the first stone, the material stone, as I am now a poor assistant again in this laying of the first formal stone, the word and sacrament, and shall ever desire to be so in the service of this place." Donne's Dedication Sermon of Lincoln's Inn Chapel. Lond. 4to. 1623, p. 21. A sermon preached by Donne in Lincoln's Inn, "preparing them to build their chapel," will be found in Donne's works, ed. by Alford, iii. 168.

then elected Dr. John Preston, one of the acknowledged leaders of the puritans, and within a few months afterwards the successor of Dr. Chaderton at Emmanuel College. Such was the favour in which Preston was held that he was allowed to regulate his attendance so that he might hold the preachership concurrently with his Cambridge mastership.

It was in this safe shelter for puritanism that Prynne entered himself to acquire a knowledge of the law. In 1623 the new chapel was completed. The members were called upon to contribute largely to the good work,[a] and did so with willingness and liberality. The fabric was completed at three times the anticipated cost, but even then the bountiful zeal of the members was not exhausted. They filled the windows with stained glass, much of which still remains. The principal members of the Inn, Lord Chief Justice Hobart, who was a great friend of Donne's, Sir James Ley, afterwards Lord Treasurer and Earl of Marlborough, Judge Richardson, Baron Denham, Sir Randolph Crewe, and others, contributed separate windows or large portions of windows; whilst seventy-five less distinguished members of the Inn filled the large west window with the emblazonment of their coats of arms. Prynne was one of these. Amongst the others were the following, whose names, like that of Prynne, are rendered familiar to us by the share they took in the public troubles of the succeeding reign: William Noy, Henry Sherfield, William Hakewill, Ralph Wilbraham, William Lenthall, Oliver St. John, and John Glyn. These were the men with whom

---

[a] "Strangers shall not know how ill we were provided for such a work when we began it, nor with what difficulties we have wrestled in the way; but strangers shall know, to God's glory, that you have perfected a work of full three times as much charge as you proposed for it at the beginning: so bountifully doth God bless and prosper intentions to his glory, with enlarging your hearts within, and opening the hearts of others abroad." Donne's Sermon on the Dedication of the Chapel of Lincoln's Inn. Lond. 4to. 1623, p. 22.

Prynne was at Lincoln's Inn, although most if not all of them were his seniors.

The chapel was consecrated on Ascension Day, 1623, by Dr. Mountain, Bishop of London. On the invitation of the Benchers, Donne worthily put a conclusion to the labour which he had begun by preaching the dedication sermon. We cannot doubt that Prynne was one of his auditors.

Whilst Prynne was pursuing his way through moots and readings and the other customary accompaniments of a course of legal study, cementing also a strong and friendly intimacy with Dr. Preston, the new preacher to his Inn, Laud was rising, although at first but slowly, towards the loftiest eminences of ecclesiastical authority. In the full flush of his victories over the Calvinists at Oxford, and the anti-ceremonialists at Gloucester, he accompanied James I. into Scotland, and was one of the English divines who assisted in the measures designed to bring about conformity between the churches of Scotland and England. His friend Bishop Neile was now advanced to the see of Durham, but neither his interest with King James nor Laud's services in the cause of Scottish uniformity, which his majesty had so much at heart, were for a long time able to prevail to raise Laud to the episcopal bench. Neile's taste led him to delight in magnificent buildings. He expended his income as Bishop of Durham with praiseworthy liberality in the improvement of the public edifices connected with the see. Durham House, his princely mansion in the Strand, shared his attention in a similar way. Under his hands it became rather a college than a single residence. In its spacious rooms were found constant "quarters" for Laud and his old friend Dr. Buckeridge, now Bishop of Rochester, as well as an occasional residence for "such learned men of Bishop Neile's acquaintance as came from time to time to attend him."[a]

[a] Heylyn's Laud, p. 67.

Durham House became indeed the head quarters of that movement-party of whom Neile and Buckeridge were the heads and Laud **the** presiding spirit. **Interest of** a more potent character than that **of Durham House was** brought to bear upon King James before he **yielded to make Laud a** bishop. "He hath a restless spirit," said **the** king, "and cannot see when matters are well, but loves to toss **and** change, and to bring things to a pitch **of reformation** floating **in** his own brain." The objection was well founded, and **proves** that James could read human character. **But he was totally devoid** of firmness. **Laud won the heart of** Buckingham. His influence was irresistible with the king, and [in] 1621 Laud was raised to the see of St. **David's.** "Take him to you," are said to have been the king's words on consenting to his nomination, "**but**, on my soul, you will repent it." Henceforth his course was clear. With Buckingham, the centre of all authority, his relations became more and more intimate. In June, 1622, he became his "confessor," and most intimate adviser in all **ecclesiastical** affairs. The death of King James in 1625 cleared away all the difficulties in Laud's path. **In** 1626 his friend Bishop Neile retired from his post of the clerk **of the closet to the** new sovereign, and procured Laud's appointment as his successor. From that time the royal ear seemed closed against every other adviser in church affairs. The coronation was committed entirely to his management, and on the 20th June, **1626, he was raised to the** bishopric of Bath and Wells.

CHAPTER IV.

PRYNNE'S FIRST BOOK.

In the time of William Prynne there was no stronger feeling in the minds of the people of England than a dread of a return of the dominion of Rome. In the estimation of our forefathers of that period popery was a conspiracy against the just liberties and the right reason of mankind. The evils connected with it as a conjoint system of belief, and of spiritual government, were deemed intolerable. In its former character, degrading superstitions seemed interwoven into its very essence; in the latter, it was seen and known to be the enemy, in every possible form, of freedom of thought, and speech, and pen; in both it was looked upon as handing over its subjects to the domination of a priesthood, who were foreigners in their hearts, whose chief allegiance was given to a foreign power, who used the people for their own purposes, kept them in ignorance as a means of perpetuating their dominion, and strove, heart and soul, by the publication of wicked libels, by secret conspiracy and open war, for the restoration of that temporal supremacy which they had lost. Many people now-a-days entertain the same opinions of the Church of Rome, but there is a marked distinction between the impression produced by these opinions upon the minds of our ancestors and upon those of our contemporaries. But there is a marked distinction between Romanism as it existed then, and now. Then, it was not merely a form of faith.

Romanism now-a-days is in multitudes of [persons] a form of faith, which leads them to an exalted but misguided piety. Such people seldom dream of the political and unpatriotic bearing of this religion; they are loyal, quiet, and sub[missive?], and are ever occupied **with** a practice of those charities to which they are led by their doctrine of merits. Romanism was then a temporal power—a power to be feared—a power for which the leading nations of Europe were ready to draw the sword, a power which could command legions although she had ceased to possess them. Besides, **the generation** amongst whom Prynne lived had **a far** more vivid impression of the real character of Rome than **we can possibly attain.** We learn that character from books, or see it as it is modified and controlled by the influence of a surrounding Protestantism; they knew it **from the** living testimony of men who had witnessed its cruelties and felt the weight of its chains. During the greater part of the **life of Elizabeth** the people had lived in a constant dread of **the** approaching resumption of the Roman sway. The queen's life was the only interposing barrier, and a profound impression of the uncertainty of that tenure was kept alive by successive conspiracies and the more direct attempts of open warfare. Even after the accession of James I. it seemed as if Roman Catholics were determined that **Protestants** should never want an excuse for believing them to be **enemies as** cruel as they were implacable. The treason of the **5th** November renewed the old impression just **as it was** beginning to fade, and fixed it indelibly upon the minds of yet more than another generation.

Some people think, it may **be, that** this dread of Rome **was** unreasonable or exaggerated. For **our** present purpose **that matters** not. It existed, and operated upon the minds of the whole nation. Prynne and all the men of his time were cradled in **it;** and they viewed all who did not partake in **it** to the **same extent** as themselves with the keenest and most watchful suspicion. Protestantism **was in** their estimation a beleaguered city. A crafty and powerful enemy was at the gates. He who broke down the defences, or sowed dissension in the garrison, was little less a public enemy than the open foe himself. Men who did the foe's work, or, in the language of the time, opened gaps at which the enemy might enter, were suspected, sometimes a little too easily, to be in communication with the foe himself. With our more perfect knowledge we may see that their suspicions were occasionally unfounded, but they cannot be deemed unreasonable, especially when grounded upon a course of conduct rather than upon a single action. Thus it is unquestionable that at the close of the reign of James I. there existed in the popular mind a deeply-rooted suspicion that it was the intention of the king and his son Prince Charles to abandon Protestantism and renew the old connection with the pope. We may safely admit that they had no such intention; but the suspicion was not unreasonable. From the death of Prince Henry the policy of King James was a series of affronts to the Protestant feelings, or it may be prejudices, of the country. The cunning and hypocritical artifices by which, whilst protesting to the contrary, he strove to overturn the Presbyterianism of his native country, and partly succeeded in doing so, generated a profound conviction of his personal insincerity. His interference to check the growing feeling in favour of a religious and not a mere holiday observance of the Sunday alarmed the people. In all parts of the country the old modes of desecrating the day were fast disappearing. The drunken festivals called " ales," with the accompanying rustic games and dances, were discontinued; men were learning to cease from their ordinary occupations; the lawyers in Lincoln's Inn, on Gataker's admonition, declined to confer with their clients or give advice on that day; the general current ran in favour of a general cessation of labour; the king endeavoured to turn back the stream and restore observances which in the minds of the people were associated with the old times before the Reformation, or with the practices of countries **not re**-formed. His interference with the course of education at **Oxford**; his anxiety to marry his son to a Spanish princess; his willingness to grant indulgences to the Roman Catholics opposed to the wishes of the parliament and people; his abandonment of the cause of his son-in-law the King of [Bohemia]; his entering into a correspondence with the pope; his patronage of Arminian clergy, although he had at one time written strongly against Arminianism; **and his** direct interference to prevent preaching against Arminianism **or** Romanism, were circumstances which sufficiently account for and justify the almost universal persuasion. When the last **of these** measures was put forth, that of interfering with preaching, the outcry was universal. Clergymen prayed publicly **to preserve the** king and prince from those who went about to withdraw them from their religion, and Dr. Donne, who had just left Lincoln's Inn, was sent to preach at Paul's Cross in order that he might assure the people, in his sermon, of his majesty's constancy in the faith. Even his eloquence was insufficient to outweigh the impression produced by the royal actions. The people thought he spoke **as if he was** not satisfied himself, and there can be little doubt that such **was the** fact.

The doctrinal Protestantism of the church during the reign of Elizabeth was unquestionably what is called Augustinian, Calvinistic, or Puritan; that is, they were the doctrines of grace in opposition **to those of free** will. These were the early doctrines of the church of Rome. But Rome, in the middle ages, wandered over to that Pelagian scheme of doctrine which she had formerly been conspicuous for opposing, and after the Reformation she held fast the new faith she had adopted more out of hatred to Calvin than out of any disregard to Saint Augustine. On the revival of the Pelagian doctrines by Arminius, at the commencement of the reign of James I., his majesty wrote against them, and sent divines to represent the churches of England and Scotland in the Synod of Dort, in which Arminianism was condemned. But in spite of royal confutation and synodal censure Arminianism soon spread widely amongst the English clergy. The divines, who insisted upon forms of worship and modes of church government as essentials of Christianity, easily adopted, as the completion of their system, a form of doctrine which explained away [justification by faith] with the equally offensive doctrines of election and predestination. Amongst the earliest to publish upon the revived Pelagian or **Arminian** side of the question was a clergyman named Richard **Mountagu**. Little is known of his early history, although his position as a principal contributor to the public **troubles** of this period might have been thought to entitle him to a place in all our collections of biography. He was a son of Laurence Montague, vicar of Dorney in Buckinghamshire. From Eton College he passed to King's College, Cambridge, in 1594, where he took the usual degrees in arts, and became distinguished for pre-eminent skill in classical and early ecclesiastical literature. Preferments dropped **upon** him in rapid succession. James I. was his special patron; besides being one of his majesty's chaplains we find Mountagu holding a canonry at Windsor, a fellowship at Eton, and the rectory of Stanford Rivers in Essex. His literary labours were of the most learned character. He corrected the proof-sheets of the Greek text of Sir Henry Savile's Chrysostom, attacked Selden upon his History of **Tithes, and** wrote upon the Christian antiquities of the earliest period ; **finally** he entered the field against the Romanists. In the parish of Stanford Rivers, some Romish priests were striving to convert one of Mountagu's parishioners. He was thus brought into a controversial dispute, in the course of which a priest sent him a pamphlet, compiled by Matthew Kellison, a priest of Douay, and entitled "A gagge for the new gospell : a briefe abridgement of the errors of the Protestants of our times." The priest accompanied this little volume with a taunting invitation to Mountagu to publish an answer, as "A good work, fit for a doctor of divinity." On his return to his books at Windsor Mountagu took the Gag "to task." The result was a volume in reply, which was published in 1624, with a preface dated from Windsor, and an announcement on the title-page that the volume was "Published by authoritie." A book thus called forth and thus published would seem unlikely to contain anything of which Protestants should complain: nor was it the less likely to please the popular taste that it was written with great asperity against Mountagu's Roman Catholic opponent. "It was ever held lawful," the author remarked, "to call a spade a spade," and "as a wise man is to be heard with attention so a fool must be answered according to his folly. And so I have answered this goodly gagger." Certainly he did not underrate the freedom of his language. The pervading tone of the whole composition is that of insolent and contemptuous defiance. Kellison, the author of the Gag, was pronounced by his replier to be "as mere a gaggler as ever grazed upon a green;" the Romish priests, who were wandering in disguise through the country, performing masses in Roman Catholic houses, and striving to make proselytes where they might safely avow themselves, were stigmatised as impostors, mountebanks, buffoons, rake-shames, and rake-hells. Theological controversialists, never unsparing in words of offence, have seldom used them more freely than Mr. Mountagu.

But that which rendered his book peculiarly unpopular was the character of his defence of the Church of England against that of Rome. He defended it as a Pelagian, or Arminian and Semi-romanist, not as an Augustinian, Calvinistic, and Protestant church. With him the Church of England allowed an authority in traditions; upheld priestly absolution; concurred with the Church of Rome on the subject of free-will; admitted " an alteration, a transmutation, or transelementation," in the consecrated sacramental elements of bread and wine; with many other doctrines nearly approximating to those of Rome. In the same year, 1624, Mountagu published another controversial treatise upon the invocation of saints, which contained many things not less repugnant to Protestant opinions.

The publication of such opinions by a royal chaplain, a clergyman known to be personally favoured by James I. and more especially their publication " by authority," excited a world of suspicion and alarm. Complaint was made to Parliament of the royal favour given to such a book. After discussion, the questions raised were referred to Archbishop Abbot, who expressed his dislike of the book and gave the author an admonition; but Mountagu, receiving encouragement from Durham house, defended himself and reasserted all his opinions in another book, entitled " Apello Cæsarem," which James I. ordered Dr. White, Dean of Carlisle, to license for publication. Whilst this appeal was in the press James I. died. Mountagu transferred his appeal to King Charles, by whom he was continued in his office of chaplain in ordinary, and then the affair rested until the meeting of Charles's first parliament.

That assembly came together in the midst of the festivities of the royal marriage. The king was universally popular, and, if the men who hated popery shook their heads when they found Henrietta Maria accompanied by a troop of priests who displayed the magnificence of their religious ceremonies with presumptuous and offensive ostentation, such men were yet willing to hope that conduct so unwise would yield to the remonstrances which it was sure to call forth. But such a time was most unfavourable for Mountagu. He who had defied the House of Commons, and disregarded the admonition of the Archbishop of Canterbury, could scarcely hope to escape with impunity. The Commons ordered him to attend at their bar. He did so. His Appeal was laid to his charge, as a book written in contempt of their previously expressed opinions and the admonition of the archbishop, and as calculated to encourage popery and to breed a jealousy between the king and his well-affected subjects. For this contempt he was committed to the custody of the serjeant-at-arms; the Archbishop of Canterbury was requested to suppress his book. Mountagu immediately appealed to the king's favourite for protection, and two days after the matter had been under discussion in the House of Commons Charles I. sent the House a message that Mountagu was his servant—his chaplain in ordinary —whom he thought entitled to as much protection as the servant of an ordinary burgess; his majesty added, that he had taken the complaint against Mountagu into his own hands; that he hoped the House would enlarge him, and that his majesty would take care and give them satisfaction. On the receipt of this message, the Speaker, apparently without the direct sanction of the House, released Mountagu on his entering into a bond for 2,000*l.* to appear when called upon. The doctrine that the king's servants were to be dealt with only by the king himself, and not by the Parliament, was highly disliked by the House, but the adjournment to Oxford on account of the prevalence of the plague procured Mountagu a respite. Ere the House reassembled the king referred his books to the consideration of a committee of bishops. Bishops * * * * *

NOTE BY THE EDITOR.

The biographical fragment which is here printed was found amongst the papers of the late Mr. Bruce. It was evidently intended to form part of a separate work, and not to make a volume of the Camden Society's publications. It is printed exactly as it stands in the MS., but it is, of course, impossible to say how far its substance or form would have been modified, if it had had the benefit of the author's last corrections.

The greater part of the documents themselves were also found amongst Mr. Bruce's papers, and were probably intended to be placed in the Appendix to the work which he contemplated. Nos. 2, 3, and 4 have been added by myself. It would be manifestly impossible to continue the biography on anything like the scale contemplated by Mr. Bruce; and I shall therefore content myself with a few incidental notices of some points in the papers themselves.

At p. 17, Cottington's statement, that Peacham confessed that he intended to preach the sermon for which he was called in question, is not without interest in relation to a celebrated case of the preceding reign, though it is possible that the acknowledgment was wrung from him by torture.

At p. 52 we have Prynne's own statement of the dates at which his book was licensed and printed. These dates fully confirm the usually received opinion, that it is impossible that the scandalous words about female actors in the Index to Histrio Mastix should have been used with an intention of reflecting upon the public performance of the Queen's Masque, which took place many weeks after the whole book had been printed. But they do not prove that Prynne had not in his mind the rehearsal of that Masque, which, as we know from Salvette's newsletters, took place almost precisely at the time when the Index was passing through the press.

At p. 87, in the account of Prynne's sufferings, will be found the correct reading of the words, " but that was a chance." Mr. Bruce in the preface to his Calendar read incorrectly, " but that was a shame," which gives quite a different tone to the passage.

Lastly, I would remark that the notices of the bargains with the City, of composition for the Londonderry fine, do not represent the final arrangement. Ultimately the lands were surrendered to the King, and the fine reduced to 12,000*l.*, which Charles had beforehand presented to the Queen.

DOCUMENTS

RELATING TO THE PROCEEDINGS AGAINST

WILLIAM PRYNNE.

DOCUMENTS RELATING TO
THE PROCEEDINGS AGAINST WILLIAM PRYNNE.

I.
THE PROCEEDINGS IN THE STAR CHAMBER.

ATTURNEY Regis versus William Pryn, Esqr. Thomas Buckner, Clarke, Michaell Sparkes, and others :

[Add. MSS. 11,764, ff. 8b—29.]

Mr. Atturney first informeth them, that **Mr.** Pryn the night before the heareing makes affidavitt, howe that hee **had done his** indeavor, and could **nott instruct his** Counsell **agaynste the heare**ing, which affidavitt being not to be beleeved in respecte of the tyme hee hath allready had, hee purposeth to lett remayne vppon the ffyle, to scandalize the Justices of the Courte, as thoughe hee had beene surprized in tyme. **Itt is ordered** to be taken off the **ffyle and** cancelled.

Bill is for writting and publishinge a scandalous and a libellous Booke **againste the State, the** Kinge, and all his people, Sheweth that Mr. **Pryn hath** beene a malignant man to the **State and** Government of the Realme, **a** mover of the **people to** discontent and sedition; and to putt this his resolution into practice hee hath compiled a booke, called *Histrio Mastix*, **the Player's** Scourge or Actor's tragedye, and therein he hath presumed to cast aspertion

CAMD. SOC. B

vppon the Kinge, the Queene, and the Common wealth, and indeavoured to **infuse an opinnyon** into **the people** that ytt **is lawfull to** laye violent handes **vppon** Princes **that** are either actors, **favourers, or spectatores of stage playes.**

All he **confesseth to** be written by himself without the helpe of any other.

For **the scandall** which is **in the booke** agaynste the Churche and **the ministers** thereof itt is **lefte outt of** the Information; and, because **he shall not** plead the **sentence heare in** excuse thereof elswhere, he **gives** him nowe **notice, that for** his **termes** of Devilles Maskes, **that Christ** is a Puritan, **as he** saith in the **799** page **of his booke, and the** other passages thereof, **he** shall not **be** heare **charged therewith, butt** take care **to right the Church, to** whome **ytt more properly** belongeth.

The booke is his accuser, and the wittnes agaynste him, beinge **the** index of **his** minde, and noe doubt butt **ytt** is his booke, and **that** that booke is **his.**

Aboute nine yeres **agoe** hee shewed a parte thereof to Mr. Doctor **Goad, and about**e vii yeres since **to** Mr. Doctor Harris, and yett in his examinacion he doth possitivlye sweare that hee never shewed the same **to** any one before hee brought itt to Mr. Buckner to be **lycensed.**

Aboute three yeres agoe the dearth was, before then the warres **were ended;** these he mencions in his booke, soe that ytt appeareth he made **the** booke **as he grewe** to be angry, and soe makes ytt swell with anger.

Mr. Atturney saith **that hee will not** make any apollogye for **stage playes,** for *Amamus tollerare multa, quæ non amamus;* he **saithe in his** booke, **that** by the statute all Stage Players are Rogues; there he fallsifyeth the statute, for ytt is onely agaynste those that wander; and by the same reason hee may call rogues all the Professors of Musicke, and soe alsoe for strollers, which in the **generall** noe man will maynteyne for truth.

Bayes in windowes, new yeres guiftes, May games, danceing, pictures in churches, &c. all he comprehendes **vnder the title of** stage playes, which **he dothe** to withdrawe the people's affection from the Kinge and Governmente. For make men beleeve **what** he saith, the consequences must nedes bee soe.

Pryns examinacion read; he confesseth hee made the booke all himselfe.

Mr. **Doctor** Goade's deposicion **reade, saith that** Mr. Pryn brought him aboute nine yeres since **a booke** agaynste stage playes, and desired to have ytt lycensed; hee vpon readinge thereof disliked ytt, and the deponent earnestlye and att large laide open **to him** the weaknes of his argumentes, and putt to him the case that yf a man in his howse were beseidged by pagans would hee nott **diguise** himselfe in his maide's apparell to escape; Pryn said he would dye fyrst; deponent said he would iustifye the contrary opinyon.

Mr. Doctor Harris read, That aboute vii yeres since Mr. Pryn brought him a treatise agaynste stage players to be lycenced to be printed, which he refused, and advertised him his argumentes were not contingentes as beinge drawne out **of** abuses of playes, which might varry **from the matter ytt selfe.**

Augustine Mathewes reade, That aboute the laste Parlament he printed some parte of the booke, att the request **of Pryn and** Sparckes.

Pryns examinacion read, That hee did nott shewe the same nor any parte thereof to any one butt Sparckes before he brought ytt to Mr. Buckner to be lycenced.

His booke is nott onely scandalous to the whole State but alsoe most idle, conteyninge in ytt most ympertinent assertions, as in his page 671 he taketh for some 7 or 8 pages followinge a greate deale of paynes to noe purpose to prove that Ste George, B$^{pp e}$ of Alexandria, was born in Capadocia.

His booke totally fraught with schisme and sedicion, his censuringe of all the people in generall, actors and spectatores of maskes and playes, of Magistrates **to indure ytt,** and **that** Kinges and **Princes that** will suffer ytt maye **iustly** therfore come to an vntymely end, which severall partes is explained by the Counsell for the Kinge, vizt. for his scandall agaynst the whole Kingdome in generall, the gentry, and the other sorte.

Mr. Masson.
Mr. Masson in his page 201: yett notwithstandinge as our Englishe ruffians are metamorphosed in their deformed frizelled lockes and hayre, so our Englishe gentlewomen, as yf they all intended to turne men outright, and weare the breeches, or to be Popishe nunnes, are nowe growne soe farr past shame, past modesty, grace, and nature, as to clipp their hayre like men, with lockes and foretoppes, and to make this whorishe cutt the verry guise and fashion of the tymes, to the eternall infamye of their sex, nation, and religion.

p. 228.
Page 228. Absolutely be expresse termes, or els by necessary consequence, condemne danceing as idolatrous, heathenishe, carnall, worldly, sensuall, and misbeseeminge Christians, and the devill himself, who danced in Herodias' daughter, was the first author of this danceing, the onely instrument that excites men to ytt, the onely person present at ytt that is honoured, pleased, and delighted by ytt.

p. 239.
5thly, daunceing, write they, is alltogether incompatible with that vniversall hollynes, modesty, temperance, gravitye, and sobriety, which God requires in all chaste and gratious Christians, ytt beinge a recreacion, as Cicero, Ovid, Virgill, &c. testifye, that none but Bedlams, drunckardes, fooles, or infamous persons vse in their ryotous voluptuous feastes, which proves ytt the verry worst and last of vices.

p. 240.
Besides it withdrawes young gentilmen from their studies to the daunceing schoole, ytt avocates young gentilwomen from their nedles and such like honest ymploymentes, and for the most parte makes them idle huswiefes, whores, or spendthriftes ever after.

p. 43.
Sixtly, they never yssued from God, or from his children, butt from the factors[a] and mynions of the devill, whoe only did frequent

---

[a] fautors?

and acte them heretofore, and aplaude, **performe, and** haunte **them** nowe.

The miserable spectatours and frequenters of these **infernall** p. 45. pleasures, they loose **their** tyme, their modesty, their honestye, **their** creditt and respecte with God, and all good men, yea, their civillitye, their chastitye, **their** money, estate, and, yf this be nott enoughe, **their** verry soules and bodye to, without repentance:

Yf any should discent from this **opinyon, this is the** censure he passeth vppon them, vizt.:

God forbedd that any whoe **have beene** dipped in the **sacred** p. 53. laver of Regineracion, any **that have beene** bathed, &c., should prove such desperate incarnate devills, such monsters **of ympiety,** such atheisticall **Judases to their lord and** Master, **such perjured** cutt throates to their Religion, such apostates or undeplored **enimyes** to their owne salvation, or such willfull bloody murtherers **to their** owne soules, as to approve or justifye or to practise these stage playes.

There are none but whores and panders **or** fowle incarnate p. 328. devills which **dare controll my** minors truthe, **which** all Christians must subscribe **vnto.**

Mr. **Recorder expresseth those** places **of this booke, which do** Mr. Recorder. traduce the governmente **of the** kingdome, **vidlt.:**

Yf **wee** somme vpp **all the** prodigall vayne expenses which p. 322. playes and play howses occasion **every** waye, wee shall finde them almost inffinite, almost incredible, alltogether intollerable in a Christian frugall State, which **must** needes abandon stage playes, which must needes ruyne many, &c.

Thereby castinge an imputacion vppon **the** State and Magistrates, as not beinge Christian or frugall in that they tollerate Playes.

This memorable Acte of suppressinge play howses, by aucthoritye p. 492. from our virtuous Queene Elizabeth and hir sage Privye Councell, as intollerable greivances **to** our cheife Christian metropolis, is an infallible argumente that they all reputed **them** insufferable corruptions in a Christian State, as **theis pyous Magistrates** demolyshed **playe** howses, and thrust out playours **from** within their libertyes, which nowe have taken sanctuarye in somme priviledged places, with^a their jurisdiction.

pp. 500, 501. I maye saffelye and conffidentlye conclude on all **the premisses** (and I **hope, &c.) that** stage playes deprave the mynde, adulterate the manners bothe of their actours and spectatours, and that therefore they are altogether vnlawffull, abominable vnto Christians, and not tollerable in any well governed Xtian common wealth, which should cause us all in generall and eache in particuler, as wee either tender the publicque or our owne private wellffare, for ever to abandone, suppresse, renounce, all stage playes. (*Crudelitas ista pietas est*) This crueltye willbee at least our pietye, in theis daungerous and wicked tymes, which crye for naught but **wrathe and vengeance:**

Whatt he meanes by suppressinge of players and pyous crueltye **in this place hee** cannot tell :—that he maye well meane to in**structe** the people to arme themselves against the State to effect it.

p. 787. That playes and players are suffered still (as to many other condempned sinnes and mischeiffes are) **it** is onely the fiaulte of Magistrates, whoe maye, whoe should, suppresse them, not of our lawes, which are most severe against them.

This needes noe exposicion, for he speaketh with open mouthe against the State.

The first fol. 560. **And maye** we not then suspect that their tolleracion of our greate resorte to stage playes hath been a great occasion of theis devowringe plagues, which formerlye and nowe of late have seised **not** onely vppon London and hir suburbes, where divers playe howses are everye daye frequented, but on other townes and cittyes? Too sure I amme that Ste Augustine, Osorius, and others, style stage playes the plague of men and manners; and that Clemens Alexandrinus, Tertullian, and Ste Chrisostome, call playe howses the state of pestilence; wee wonder therefore **yf they produce a** plague in those kingdomes and cittyes which permitt them:

---

^a without ?

which should lessen all playe poetts to give over their com- fol. 563.
poseinge, all common actors, &c., all Christian Princes, Cittyes,
States, and Magistrates, whose connivencye at any evill which they
might suppresse doth make them deeplye guiltye of them for
ever to exile playes and devilishe playe howses, for feare they pull
downe Godes judgments downe uppon them, as they have uppon
others.

Ut quis potest occidere, peritia est, ars est, usus est. *Scelus non* A marginall
tantum geritur, sed docetur. Quid potest inhumanius, quid acerbius note in f. 519.
*dici? disciplina est, ut quis perimere possit; et gloria est, quod
peremit.* Cyprian, Epist. li. 2, Epist. 2 Donato. See Onus
Ecclesiæ, c. 28, sect. 7, 8, which we maye well applye to our
tymes.

How iustlye maye hee applye theis thinges to our tymes lett all
the kingdome iudge, but maye bee hee will saye hee meant his
applicacion to the last quotation of Onus Ecclesiæ. Mr. Recorder
produces that booke, the quoted place is read, and it is worse, yf
worse maye bee, then the quotation of Cyprian.

Noe playe howses are to bee suffered by the Jesuites' sentence, p. 1002, a mar-
whose reasons I wishe all magistrates and others would consider. ginall note
vpon Joannes
Butt, because all men heere neglect their dutye, God himselfe Mariana the
will att one tyme or other finde out a meanes whereby he will cast p. 481.
out theis plagues, not without somme publicque calamitye, as the
prophett threatened to Ninivee.

Whether he meanes hereby that God should arme the people
against the magistrates, and soe make a publicque callamitye, whoe
knowes:

Out of Boden. But there is noe hope of seeinge playes for- p. 484.
bidden by the Magistrates, for commonlye they are the first att
them.

This is nott in Boden's Latin coppie, which is shewed in Courte
by Mr. Recorder.

8   DOCUMENTS RELATING TO THE

Mr. Sollicitor. For and **conscerninge** his Scandalles and Aspertions, layde vppon the Kinges howse and **Courte**, Mr. Sollicitor declares it, **vidlt :**

pp. 47, 48.   Whie **doe men send** for stage players to their howses, whie **doe** they **flocke vnto their** theaters thicke and three fould on festiuall and **solempne seasons,** especiallye in the Christmas tyme, [if] it is not **out of worldlye** pomp and **state, out of** a prodigall and vayne-glorious **humour, a** degenerous **and** unchristian simbolizacion with the **present world,** to banishe **God and** Christe out **of our** hartes, grace **out of our** Soules? &c.

p. 360, a marginal note.   Note this well:—ye lascivyous **persons,** whoe harbour **players in** your private howses.

p. 58.   Or can you bee soe besotted **by the** devill (as alas to **manye are) as to thincke** to please, **to** honnour, courte, or entertayne Christe **Jesus,** to welcomme him into the world, to celebrate his natiuitye with infernall stage playes, **the verye** monumentes **and** ensignes **wherewith the** Pagans did courte their devill godes?

p. 743.   Alas, into what atheisticall heathenishe tymes are **wee nowe relapsed** into, what stupendeous height of more then **Pagan** impietye **are wee** nowe degenerate, when, as Stage playes, **the** verye cheiffest pompe and ornaments of the most execrable Pagan Idolles feastivytyes **are** thought the necessarye appendantes of **our** most holie Christian solempnityes.

When as wee cannot sanctiffye **our Lordes** daye, or observe a 5ᵗᵒ of Nouember, &c., or suche solempne feastes, or Christmas (as wee phrase **it), in a** plausible **pyous sorte (as to** manye Paganizeinge Christians conceipt it), **without drinckinge,** roreing, &c., maskes, and stage playes.

The first fol. 558.   Hee **makes** an applicacion of a disaster by fyer which beffell in the **Corte of** Charles the **sixt of** fraunce, in theis wordes,

Sure I amme it was the iuste judgmente of God to **teache kinges and greate** men not to **bee** actours or spectatours **of vanitye, but wholie to laye** aside such foolishe maskes or enterludes.

Hee **makes** another **applicacion out of** Lampridius Œlius, his storye of Heliogabalus, his acteinge of Venus parte in an **enterlude** abonte Paris and the Apple, in theis wordes:

An apparante proofe that an emperour daunceinge, or acteinge p. 856. a parte in playes or maskes, even in his owne private pallace, **is** infamous, and his resorte to play howses more abhominable.

I conceyve **that** common stage playes, to which every cobler, p. 734. tyncker, whore, and base mechanicke, **maye resorte every** daye, as many of them doe, are noe **meete sportes or** entertaynments for Christian princes, states, and potentates, &c.

And in the page followinge, videlicet, And can any one then bee p. 735. soe braynesicke, soe shamelesse to affirm that theis anathematized heathenishe spectacles, theis stigmatized varletts, which **all** tymes, all Christians, all men of gravitye and wisdome, have disdayned as the most lewde, infamous persons, are fitt to entertayne the noblest princes, or to appeare before them in their **royall pallaces in tyme** of greatest state.

None delight in common spectacles but such **as** would be spec- First, **fol. 539,** tacles. a marginall note.

Hee quoteth **a place out** of Eneas Sylvius, a most scandalous one, p. 737. layeinge most insufferable aspertion uppon the Kinges courte, in theis wordes, *Quod si tempus disserendi daretur, monstrarem **omnes** homines stultos esse, qui vitam habentes, aliam in qua possint honeste vivere, in Curiis principum se præcipitant. Ideo vos tantum moneo, ut agrum hunc histriones et adulatores, ac alios nebulones metere sinatis, qui nigrum in candida vertunt. Nullus enim veris bonis apud Principes locus, nulla emolumenta laborum.*

And in page 738 hee goeth further, videlicet, That stage p. 738. players, tumblers, **fidlers,** singers, jesters, and such like idle persons have followed princes courtes and haunted greate mens howses; that they have there founde accesse and harboure, when as experienced, vertuous, well deservinge men have beene **excluded,** contempned, and sent a waye without rewarde. **Theis** catterpillers and pestes of the common weale not onely anticipateinge in the meane while their charitye to the poore and bountye to men of desert, but even exhausteinge their treasures, depraveinge their manners, foementinge their **vyces**, to the publicque preiudyce and **their owne** eternall **perdition.**

<small>p. 811</small> And, **not content** with this, hee will tell you what devynes or chapleynes **his Matie** doth entertayne, videlicet, Did **not** Amazias the **priest of Bethel** accuse the propheett Amos to Kinge Jeroboam, for conspireinge against him, in the middest of the howse of Israell? And that the lande was not able to beare his wordes, which **scandalous** accusacion not succeedinge, did hee not there-uppon advise him to flye into the lande of Judah, and eate breade and **prophesie** there, chargeinge him lyke an episcopall comp-troller not to prophesie any more att Bethell, for it was the Kinges chapple and **the** Kinges courte, where hee would have noe faith-full prophettes, noe truth tellinge, sinne rebukeinge chapleynes **comme, whoe** knowe not howe to flatter, &c.

<small>Pryn's owne wordes.</small>

Yf hee had possitively named his Matie in theis places his **meanynge** would have been to playnne, therefore he names other **princes, and** leaves the applicacion to the reader.

<small>Sir John Finche.</small> Next, Sr John Finche chardgeth him with what conscernes the Queenes person, and after some speeche of the nature of the booke, and the excellencye of hir Royall Matie, sheweth howe their lo^pps had, the former daye, heard this monster of men and nature spitt his venome against the people in generall, the magistrates, and his Maties howse and houshould, they shall nowe see him spitt his **venome att** the throane it selfe. And soe [he] begins att Mr. Pryns **endeavo**r to cast a generall aspertion uppon hir M^ties nation in a marginall note, in page 414, in theis wordes.

In imitacion of theis, some Frenche woemen, or monsters rayther, in Michas Terme 1629, attempted to acte a Frenche playe att the playehowse in Blacke Friers, an impudent, shamefull, grace-lesse, yf not more than whorishe attempte.

Then in his Index he comes neerer to the end of his mallyce, in the tytle Woemen, where hee saieth, Woemen actours, notoryous **whores.** And dare then any Christian woman bee soe whoreishlye impudent as to acte or speake publicquelye on a stage, **perhappes** without hayre, and in man's apparrell, in the presence of sundrye men and woemen. (*Dii talem terris avertite pestem.*)

Fowerthlye, daunceing, say they, even in Queenes themselves and in the verye greatest persons, whoe are commonlye the most devoted **to it, have been** all wayes scandalous and of ill reporte amonge the saintes of God, &c. **And for his** author of this hee scites Theophilact, Enarr[ationes] uppon Math. 14, page 34, whoe onely there speackes of Herodias daughter in particuler, by whose abuse of daunceinge Ste John Baptiste was beheaded, and yett the mallyce of this monster will applye that to these tymes.

p. 236.*

Delight and skill in daunceinge, a badge of lewde lascivyous woemen and strumpettes.

Index, daunceing.

Thus farre the Waldenses and Albigenses, whose wordes I would the daunceinge wantons (that I say not whorishe), Herodiasses, the effeminate cincqua-pace, coranto friskinge gallantes of our age, together wth our rusticque hoblinge satyres, nymphes, and daunceinge fayeries, whoe spend their strength, their tyme, especiallye the Easter, Whitsontyde, &c. in lewde lascivyous daunceinges, would nowe seriouslye consider.

By Herodias, whome he meante, his mallyce maye easelye discover him, and soe leaves him with the attributes hee gives himselfe in his verses, in the beginninge of his booke,

> Omnia sunt suspecta tibi, quia publicus hostis
> Et majestatis diceris esse reus.

And soe hopes their lo^{pps} will conceyve him *Reus Læsæ Maiestatis.*

Mr. Attourneye chargeth him with the crymes and assertions against the Kinges person, videlicet, hee would make him worse than Neroe, vizt. London play howses beinge soe muche augmented nowe as that all **the** devilles chappelles, beinge fyve in number, maye **not contayne them, when as** wee **see a** sixt **nowe**

Mr. Attourney first Epist. dedicatorye.

---

* 136 in MS.

added to them, whereas in vitious Neroes raigne there was but three standinge **theaters** in pagan Rome.

p. 320.   Neyther **neede** I seeke for further testimoneyes in soe **cleare** a case, since **our owne** domesticque experience, especiallye in Kinge Henry **8, whoe spent** infinite somes of monye vppon stage playes, maskes, **and such** prodigall shewes and pageantes.[a]

Not to mencion the over prodigall disbursements vppon playes and **maskes** of late penuryous tymes, which have been well nighe as expensive as the warres.

p. 856.   After a longe storye out of Herodian aboute the Emperour Antoninus his **love of** stage playes, hee passeth in his owne charracter this sentence uppon him, Soe execrable did his daunceinge, acteinge, **effeminacye,** and love of stage playes make hem to all the

p. 755.   senate and people, that they thought him unworthie to raigne or lyve, **and at last** dragged his carckesse throughe the cittye, and cast it into the common jakes.

First, he findes faulte with the tymes, the people, the magistrates, **and the** Kinge and Queene themselves; then hee goeth **aboute to** directe a waye to remedy it, not by precept, for that **would** bee to playne, but hee goeth aboute by example to doe it, sheweinge the lyfe and death of princes that loved stage playes.

p. 966.   Johannes Mariana the Jesuite, whose worckes have been long since **condempned as** most seditious, **hee** commendes to the uttermost, **and concludes** in his wordes:

p. 848.   **Neyther is** the acte **or** publicque profession of acteinge stage **playes vile and** execrable onely when it is practised for lucre sake, **but lykewise** the voluntarye personateinge of them to for recreacion or entertaynemente, especiallye in persons of rancke and quallitye. To instance some:

First, **it** hath been allwayes reputed dishonorable, shamefull, infamous, **for** emperours, **kinges,** or princes, to **come upon** a

---

[a] "**is a** sufficient confirmation of my minors truth" **follows** in the printed book.

theater, or acte a parte in a private or publicque enterlude, to delight themselves or others.

Hence Dion Cassius, &c. impute it an unexpicable **infamye** to Caius Caligula, whoe by publicque edicte caused the **people** to bee present att his enterludes, &c., which caused Chœrea to murther him as hee **came from the theater, an** end suitable to his vitious, tyrannicall playe adoreinge lyfe.

Of **Neroe:** Such was the playerlyke, **citharedicall lyfe of** this p. 852. vitious emperour, which made **him soe execrable to some** noble Romanes, that to vindicate the honnor **of** the Romane empire, which was thus basely prostituted, they conspired his distrucion.

Of **Commodus: howe hee** was poysoned by Electus and Martia, p. 854. which severall passages **are** most pregnante testimonyes howe infamous and disgracefull it is for kinges or emperours **to turne** actors, maskers, &c.

Tribellius Policarpus[b] recordes that Gallienus the Emperour was p. 465.[a] murthered by Marcianus, Heraclianus, and Claudius, for this verye cause, least by his lewde example in frequentinge stage playes and favoringe stage players, with which he had filled his pallace, hee should bringe himselfe and the Republicque into ruyne.

Theis severall kinges and emperours stage delightes **beinge** thus the just occasions of their untymelye deathes.

In all which passages, thoughe not in expresse tearmes, yet by examples and other implicite meanes, hee laboures to infuse an **opinyon** into the people, that for acteinge or beinge spectatours of playes or maskes it is just and lawfull to laye violent handes uppon kinges and princes.

xv° Februarii, 9 *Caroli.*

All the first named lordes beinge present but my Lord Keeper; Marquess Hambleton **beinge** there present, **and absent the** first daye,

---

[a] 555 in MS. [b] See **Trebellius Pollio**, in *Histriomastix*, p. 465.

The defendents counseles, havinge obtayned this tyme to consider of the defence, goe to it, vidlt.:

Mr. Holborne.   Mr. Holborne.—His harte will **not give** him leave **to** saye **that** Mr. Pryn is guiltye of suche fowle thinges as are layde against him, in such nature as they are alleaged and construed, but hee confesseth that in his tearmes and invectives hee hath much offended, and Mr. Attournye hath done but justlye in prosecuteinge against him.

For that exception is taken to **him that** hee, beinge noe devyne, meddled with thinges out of his vocacion, hee doth not conceyve it meerely proper for devines to wryte of such a subjecte, for manye laye men have alsoe written against stage playes.

For the other matter treated of in his booke, besides stage **playes,** hee doth not conceyve they are altogether *dehors*, but are **some one way or** other pertinent.

Hee is hartelye sorrye that his style hath been soe tarte, bitter, and transported, and it may bee gathered that hee did not thincke such construction would bee made thereof by that, that hee brought the booke **to** Mr. Buckner to bee lycensed, and it was by him allowed, and hee thinckes there were never any brought here in judgemente but for bookes unlycenced.

Itt was not printed beyounde the seas, nor in corners, nor unlycensed, nor privately dispeirced; and yf Mr. Pryn had conceyved that there had been in it any thinge **of** that construction, which hee doth confesse that the same may be wrested to, hee would **never** have soe publicquelye avowched; and all that in the particulers **hath** been **scited** against him is not possitive from himselfe, **but as** consequence of thinges written by other authours.

And whereas he is taxed to have sworne that he **never shewed** this booke to any but Sparckes before it came to Mr. Buckner **to** bee lycenced, contrarye to the deposicion of Doctor Goade and Doctor Harris, it was a **booke of** the same nature, **and not the** same **booke, the** firste beinge but of a quier **of** paper, **and this** of a **greate** vollume.

Mr. Atkins.—Hee will nott offerr any thinge in defence, but hee will expresse that those thinges which the ingenuity of the Kinges councell hath made to beare a hard sence are not possitive from the authour, but as consequentes of what others have spoken; as such as goe to playes are incarnate devills, it is not meerely his wordes, but the collection from others.

That our Englishe ladyes have cast awaye all virtue, modestye, &c., hee doth not saye soe of all ladyes, but those who spend all their tyme in playes.

For daunceing, hee hath onely condempned wanton, uncivill, amorous daunceinge, and hee doth beleive it was farre from him to compare the tymes or person of Nero to his Matie or governmente: hee cannot condempne his harte, neyther will hee excuse his indiscretion, and soe leaves him to their lo^{pps} mercye.

Mr. Herne.—Hee himselfe hath cleared himselfe, as muche as any waye maye be spoken for him, which is the intencion of his harte explained in his answere and examinacion, and noe man cann explayne a man's owne harte better then himselfe.

Itt is true hee hath offended the common people, the magistrates, the Queene, and the Kinge; and that cann bee spoken for him is, that hee and all his councels maye bee suitors to their lo^{pps} to consider him, as hee hath explained himselfe in his answere, for, as hee oweth him servyce as a counsell, hee oweth himselfe that duetye not to forfeyte his discretion for a clyent.

Mr. Buckner in his defence saith, hee lycenced but 64 pages of it; that that was not lycenced to bee published, but onely att the request of Sparckes to bee entered into the Stationers' Hall, to intitle Sparckes to the sale of it; that hee advised the booke should not bee published, and said to Sparckes, he would loose his cares yf hee published it; that when it was published, by his meanes warrant was obtayned from the late Lord B^{pp} of Canterburye for calling in of the same.

17 *Februarii*, anno 9 *Car.*

Lord Treasurour	**Lord** Wimbleton
Lord of Canterburye	B{^{pp}} of London
Lord of Yorcke	Lo: Newburghe
Lo: Privye Seale	**Sir** Tho: Edmondes
Lo: Ma: Hambleton	Sir Henry Vane
Lord Arundell	**Sir** Thomas Jermyne
Lord Pembrooke	Secretarye Cooke
Lord of Suffolke	Secret: Windebancke
Lord Dorsett	Lord Richardson
Lord Exon	Lord Heath
Lord Carlisle	Lord Cottington.

Lo. Cottington.

His Ma{^{ties}} attourneye generall hath brought this man **to** judgmente **for** publisheinge a libellous booke against his Ma{^{tie}} and the state, and it is in manner against all mankinde, and the best of mankinde, as kinges, queenes, **princes**, &c., yea, in **a** manner against all thinges. Hee **thinckes Mr.** Pryn did not invent this booke alone, but was assisted by the devill himselfe, and it is not **the first booke** of this nature hee made, for hee made one booke against the due reverence of our Saviour, which none but a devill would doe. This booke **is to** effecte disobedyence to **the Kinge,** disobedyence to the state, and a generall dislyke unto all governmente.

For the condicion **of the** partye, what oathes and affidavittes hee makes, first sweares one thinge in his aunswere, then another **thinge in** his examinacion, then makes falce affidavittes.

The truthe is, Mr. Pryn would have a newe churche, newe government, a newe kinge, for hee would make the people altogether offended with all thinges att the present.

Itt is said, hee had noe ill intencion, noe ill harte, but hee maye bee ill interpreted. That must not bee allowed him in excuse, for he should not have written any thinge that would **beare** construccion, **for hee** doth not accompanye his booke, to **make** his intencion knowne to all **that reades it.**

When hee considers those **thinges of** highe nature in his booke against the Kinge, the Queene, and the state, hee **cannott but** admyre his Maties mercye in **bringinge** him to soe easye **an accompt** for it.

Pecham **had his studdye** searched, where there was founde a lybellous sermon **against the Kinge,** which hee confessed hee did intend **to preache at the Assizes.** Hee was arraigned and convicted of treason. **Thereuppon hee did not publishe it.**

This man hath published and stoode in justificacion of a farre more lybellous and seditious booke, therefore it is high tyme to **cut** of him that hath endeavoured to make such dissention and distraccion in the kingdome; therefore hee condempneth the booke to bee in a most ignominyous manner burnte by the hande **of the hangman, that Pryn bee degraded of all degrees, eyther att the Universitye or Innes a Courte,** to stand on the pillorye **att Westminster and Cheape side, to loose** an eare att eyther place, to weare papers declareinge **his offence, and to bee perpetuallye** imprisoned, and paye a fyne of 5000^{li}.

Mr. Buckner—Little is said **against him by Mr.** Attournye, but it doth appeare hee eyther lycenced, or began to lycence it, and **a** greate inconvenyence hath befallen the state by his neglect **in not suppressinge it att the** beginninge, fynes him 50^{li}.

For Sparckes — hee was the first broacher of this booke, he sollicited the printinge, **hee did** publishe it, would barter and sell the same after they were called in, and is proved to offende often tymes **in this** nature. Therefore hee to paye 500^{li} fyne, to stand **in the pillorye with papers, and** imprisonment at the Kinges pleasure; **the three printers** acquitted.

The booke maye justlye be called lybellous, scandallous, **and** Lo. Heath. seditious ; Mr. Pryn **is the** author and publisher, Sparckes the stationer and publisher, Mr Buckner charged **to bee** the lycencer, Aldee, Jones, and Cotes **the** printers. The **three last,** noethinge **beinge** proved against them, hee acquiteth; Mr. Buckner hee conceyveth **was** abused by Sparckes and Pryn, **and his** hande subtiblye gotten to parte of the booke; but hee was to blame that hee would bee abused, and in those 64 pages to which his hande, **is** there is not any thinge **for** which hee will sentence him; **in** respecte whereof, and of Mr **Buckner's** fayer carryage and conformitye other **wayes, hee will leave** him with a *non liquett.*

For Mr. Pryn—**hee** hath compiled and published a volluminous lybell, but more properly a scandalous and seditious booke. Yf hee medled with is owne profession, it had been well, but that supposed learninge and zeale wherewith **hee was** inflamed must soe farre transporte him that hee will take uppon to bee the revenger of the present injuryes of the tyme, and yf this booke and author doe **not** sufferr, the whole kingdome must needes sufferr. Forme or **order** in his booke there is not any, it is all full of confusion; hee scites authors one halfe whereof he doth beleeve hee hath not **in** his studdye; hee hath forgotten the first pointe of religion, charitye, for hee expresseth such **virrulent** rayleinge as noe religious man would doe.

The ayme of this booke seemeth to bee againste stage playes, but hee hath involved therein musicke, daunceinge, new yeares guiftes, and all thinges els that came **in** his waye, and sure it is a greate want of judgment to condempne those thinges in the generall which in themselves are indifferent.

Hee hath not done this without premonition of reverend devines, Doctour Goad and Doctour Harris, but hee followed the humours of manye whoe yf they cann but wryte will not rest tyll they publishe **themselves** fooles in printe.

Butt that whereuppon hee shall grounde his sentence are those which in his booke[a] soe expresslye layde that for them it would have been noe strayne of lawe to have him arraigned for highe treason.

Hee casteth a generall aspertion uppon the ladyes, speakinge of longe hayre, which our Englishe ladyes, whoe have cast of God and nature, shame and modestye, are nowe ashamed of, as beinge out of fashion.

    [a] Perhaps " grounds which, in this book, are, &c."

For the magistrates, he condempnes them generallye, **that it is their wante of care that theis abuses are sufferred, and yf a magis**trate bee once brought into **contempte there is** noe obedyence to bee expected.

Daunceinge in queenes themselves allwayes held of ill repute.

Page 856. "**An** apparante proofe **that** an emperour seeinge a maske or dauncinge is infamous."

P. 320. " Neyther neede wee seeke further testimonye in soe **cleare a case,**" &c.

That the prodigall disbursementes of late penurious tymes have been more expencesive then the warres; a most infamous and abhominable lye.

The common people, when they read his booke, **they will take** him to bee a man of judgment and beleive him, **and with what** hearte will they paye subsidyes and duetyes, when they are made beleive they are thus expended, and in that he hath made the Kinge guiltye of infamye and robbinge the people?

Then page 555. Theis emperours beinge the iust occasion of their owne deathes, for to taxe the person of a kinge to bee infamous for daunceinge, or seeinge a maske or playe, and then **by** examples to give intimacion of the lawfullnes of murtheringe for the same, a cryme of the highest nature.

All his excuse is, that it was lycenced; yf it were, it cannott excuse him, for an author whoe taketh uppon him to wryte ought **to** bee a man judicyous to understand whatt hee wrytes; butt he is of opinyon it was not lycenced.

Statutes of 21 Ed. 3. condempned them that disperced lyes and tales to bee imprisoned tyll they founde the author; this man hath noe author but himselfe, therefore perpetuall imprisonmente.

For the same, 12 Ric. 2. cap. 11, great punishmente **such as the** Kinges councell should thincke fitt.

1 & 2 Phill. & Marye, pillorye and loss of **cares** for seditious **newes.**

1 of Eliz., revived in the xxiii° Eliz.

For his fower fould offence against the ladyes, magistrates, Kinge, and Queene, 4000^{li}, vidlt., a 1000^{li} a peece, and perpetuall imprisonmente.

Hee hath been a scandall to lawe and learninge, therefore direccion to the Universitye and Innes of Courte to degrade him, then to stande in the pillory att Cheape side and Westminster, &c.

Sparckes, 500^{li}, the bookes to bee burnte by the hangman, and Sparckes to stand by Pryn with a booke in his hande, readye to deliver to the hangman to burne.

Lo. Richardson.

Since hee had the **honnour to** attend this **Courte** much complainte hath been aboute wryteinge and printeinge of **bookes,** for hee findes the ould verse true,

Scribimus **indocti doctique poemata** *passim:*

for this booke hee **cann tearme it** noethinge but *Monstrum horrendum informe,* **ingens,** a most huge, scandalous, infamous, and seditious lybell against the Kinge and Queene, such as the eye of man never sawe, nor the eare of man ever heard. It is scandalous to all the people of the kingdome; he observeth in the Epistle to the reader more, "Because I observed the number of playes and playehowses to increase daylie," " Shakespeare's Plays printed in better paper then Bibles", " **above 40,000** playe bookes printed and **vented** within this two yeares, and finde better vent then sermons," all to laye an aspertion uppon **the state,** in neglectinge religion and furtheringe playes, &c.

This monster spittes **noethinge but** venome, and that att every man ; **the** gunpowder traytors would blowe the state into the ayer, and this man will **dampne them all** to hell.

Hee doth not **onely** condempne playes and players, but all that come there and every thinge done there ; daunceinge is the devilles procession, and soe **many** paces as a man paceth in daunceinge soe manye steppes hee is forward to hell ; and that christians ought not to learne their **children to** daunce.

The hartes and **good** opinyon **of** a subjecte is the Kinges best treasure, and for a man to endeavour to defraude the Kinge of this treasure is a most damnable offence, and yf hee were to **bee tryed** therefore before him, **in** the places where hee sittes, under **the** Kinges favour hee would give it another name.

Pryn wrytes that Neroes frequentinge of playes was the cheifest occasion that caused Sabrius [a] Flavius to conspire his death, least the common wealthe, addicted to playes, should bee overthrown.

His tearmes and attributes which hee gives to Neroes conspiratours are, that they were noble and worthie, and did it to vindicate the honnour of the empire, which worth and noblenes hee meerelye antributes to them in respecte **hee did thincke the** conspiracye to bee worthie **and noble. Hee hath forsaken** God and his alleagiaunce to the Kinge and Queene, and charitye to all the people.

Agreeth in the sentence with my Lorde Cottington—the bookes to bee burned in Cheapeside or Paules Churchyarde, to bee expelled the barre, to bee degraded att the Universitye and Innes of Courte, to stand on the pillorye att, &c., and loose his eares, fyne 5,000li, perpetuall imprisonmente, to have nethyr incke nor paper, but as manye Prayer Bookes as hee will, to make recognicon of his offence in this courte, at Cheapeside, and Westminster.

For Sparckes—hee agrees with my Lorde Cottington. **For Mr.** Buckner hee is a grave and reverend devyne, and doth beleive was abused by Pryn and Sparckes; whether he allowed the booke or noe doth not appeare; *non liquett*.

Aldee, Jones, and Cotes he dismisseth—the other three hee will sentence. Se. Windebancke.

Mr. Buckner hee doth beleive did lycence the booke—sentenceth him 200li fyne, imprisonmente dureinge the Kinges pleasure.

Sparckes a notoryous offender; fyne 1,000li, pillorye with papers, and disabled ever to sell bookes.

For Pryn, more worthie of a halter then a sentence in **this** courte ; hee hath opened his mouthe as wyde as hell, againste **the** Kinge,

---

[a] Sabinus.

Queene, magistrates, and all the kingdome ; fyne 10,000[li] and imprisonmente, and corporall punishmente, with my Lord **Cottington**, and the bookes to bee burnte.

Sec. Cooke.

For Mr. Pryn—it seemeth hee read more then hee studdied, and that hee wrytt more then he considered.

When wisdome is mixed with a man's owne humour yf it bee to farre strayned it often falleth out to the destruction of the aucthor and others. Vyce is both to bee reprehended and punished, but for a temporall man to imploye his tallent in that waye, which belongeth not unto him, not bee tollerated. It is not his intencion nor **meaninge, nor** (as hee thinckes) is it the meaninge of any of their lo[pps], to appollogize for stage playes, but this booke is not meerely against stage playes, but it rayther quarrells with all mankinde, and Mr. Pryn, lyke madd Ajaxe beinge offended with Ulisses and the **Grecian** princes, whippes all that come in his waye, and hee conceyveth **his** Ma[tie] greatlye extended his mercye towardes him in bringeinge him to soe easye a tryall.

Sentence, Mr. Pryn, as my Lord Cottington did.

Sparckes and Buckner, with the Judges.

Hee is sorrye Mr. Pryn is a gentleman, sorrye hee is of that honnorable profession and societye that hee is of.

Sir Thomas Jermyn.

Hee hath compared the heathenishe playes with Christian recreacions; hee cannot thincke him but worthie of severe sentence; he **castes** aspertion uppon all sortes of people, yea, uppon the throane **it selfe; hee** maketh the Kinge the greatest offender; and what **manner of** Kinge is hee whome he thus traduceth? no Saule, noe Ahab, **but a** kinge in whome Adam hath not sinned, and maye well **bee** compared with the best of men.

This man's zeale hath soe overflamed, that there is not by him any recreacion att all **lefte for Christians,** but, as yf hee had in his handes **the** opinyon of devynes, aucthors, and councells, condempnes every thinge in his owne fancye. If hee had kepte his booke **in** his studdye, and enjoyed the singularitye of his owne **opinyon, his** offence had not been soe exorbitant; in alleadginge the examples of vitious kinges, by **him scited in his booke**, the venomme of his harte passeth by all their vyces, attributes their untimelye deathes **to be** justlye occasioned **for** allowinge **stage** playes.

For Mr. Buckner, hee doth not soe fullye apprehend his offence as that hee **dare** sentence him, therefore hee agreeth for him, and the rest alsoe, with my Lord Heath.

Itt appeares Mr. Buckner did lycence 64 pages of **the** booke, and Sir Hen. Va that within the said 64 pages there is verye ill passages, therefore sentenceth him 200^{li} fyne and imprysonmente accordinge to the course of the Courte.

Sparckes published **and** disperced the whole volume, with a **desire of gayne**, knowinge **the same to** contayne most seditious matters, and that but 64 pages was lycenced; **fynes him a 1000^{li}**, and corporall punishmente. Agreeth with my **Lord Cottington**.

For Mr. Pryn there is noe difficultye in the **case**, for **his** cryme is most manifest in frameing and publishinge a booke which is mearelye a context, full of sedition, **annimateinge the** people to withdrawe their allegiaunce from the Kinge; his scandalous and opprobrious language (yf **the** matter had **not been soe** haynous) might have been better dispenced withall, but **it is the** ordinarye style of all wryters of his kinde. In his sentence concurres with my Lord Cottington, for his degradinge att the Universitye and the Innes a Courte: his fyne, pillorye, looseinge his eares, imprysonmente, **and** that he make a recognicion of his offence; and for **the other** passages of his booke, touchinge the Churche, leaves him **to receyve** his punishmente in **the** Highe Commission Courte, and his affidavit to be taken of the fyle and cancelled.

Mr. Pryn taketh uppon him to forme a newe **kinde of govern-** Sir Thomas **mente** and doth denounce all **that** bee not of **his** opinyon to bee Edmondes. reprobates and lymbes of **the** devill. When he considers the enormitye of Pryn's offence, **he** is hartelye sorrye that this Courte cannott doome him to sufferr accordinge **to the** quallitye of his offence—concurres in his sentence with the **highest**.

For Mr. Buckner, hee doth **conceyve it** was his misfortune to bee overreached by Pryn and Sparckes; therefore **thinckes** him onely worthie of a sharpe reprehencion.

Sparckes, **the** pryme publisher **of this** booke, hath **dyvers** tymes offended **in** the lyke nature; fyne, 1000^{li}, and in corporall punishmente agreeth with my Lord Cottington.

Newburghe. **Agreeth with** my Lord Cottington.

Bpp. London.[a] Hadd this scurrilous, virrulent, and infamous libell founde vente, the next booke would have been meere treason:

He condempnes the booke to the fyer, and the **author and publisher**, with **my** Lord Cottington.

Mr. Buckner—*Non liquett.*

Carlisle,
Wimbleton,   } Concurre with my Lord Cottington.
Exon,

Dorsett. **The** publicque callamitye and misserye which this Minor Prophett Pryn hath denounced against **us** is sooner to be expected for sufferinge such men as hee to lyve amongst us then for any other thinge. No man ever hath condempned heresie with more bitter invectyves than this man hath censured mankinde. Christ sent his disciples with *Ite prædicate*, and they did accordinglye preache, teache, and practyze charytye and obedyence; but the devill, on the contrarye parte, wrought alsoe miracles, and scited Scriptures to wicked endes, and sendes out his disciples with *totum prosternite mundum;* and this man, forsakeinge Christes rule, as one of the devilles faithfull agentes, followes his instruccions:

This man wilbe affrighted at a three-cornered capp, sweate att a surplus, sighe to heare musicke, swounde to the signe of the crosse, yett will make noe conscyence to lye, forsweare, and perjure him selfe, and for the advantage of the common cause to rayle uppon the Kinges estate, and instructe treason. Hee is all purple within, **all pryde,** all mallyce, all spite.

[a] Bishop Juxon.

For his scandall of the Queene, rayther impietye then ingratitude; a Queene, in whose prayse it is impossible **for a poett** to fayn, **or** orator to flatter.

Yett this man, lyke a madd dogge, bayes at the **moone**. It **is** not Mr. Attournye, but mankinde, **that** hath brought him to judgmente, for **there is noe** man that hath escaped his lashe.

Sentenceth him 10,000^{li} fyne, to stand on the pillorye, and to have his eares cropped, but, because **to cover his shame** hee will dispence with his conscyence and weare a peryewigge, hee would have his nose slitt, and marcked in the forehead; that the bookes bee burnt, and a proclamacion to call them all in.

Sparckes, as **my Lord Cottington,** and to bee disabled **from** selling bookes more.

For Mr. Buckner, hee makes a difference betweene **negligence** and wickednes. *Non liquett.*

Concurres with my Lord of Dorsett.   Suffolke.

With my Lord Cottington, acquites Mr. Buckner.   Pembrooke.

For Mr. Pryn, with the highest.   **Arundell.**

For Sparckes, with Mr. Comptroller. **And for** Mr. Buckner, hee hath heard never otherwise then well of him, and hee is sorrye hee cannott concurre with some of their lo^{pps} in excuseinge him, but all he findes in **this case** against him, **hee cannott but sentence** him 100^{li} fyne.

Though hee hath been absent **the first daye,** yett for the tyme Ma. Hamble-hee satt he findes the cause **soe odyous that** hee agreeth in his $^{ton.}$ sentence with the highest.

The booke to be burnte, the aucthor to paye 5000^{li} fyne, to Prinye Seale.[a] stande on the pillorye, to loose his eares, imprisonmente dureing the Kinges pleasure, the exhibittes and affidavittes to bee taken of the fyle and cancelled.

Buckner and Sparckes, with my Lord Cottington.

For Sparckes and Mr. Buckner, hee agrees **with my** Lo. Cot- Ep'us Ebor.[b] **tington.**

[a] The Earl of Manchester.   [b] Archbishop Neile.

Pryn, the aucthor of a lybellous, treasonable, and volluminous booke, wherein he doth, lyke madd Ajax, as Mr. Secretarye Cook hath said, **takeinge** occasion to **fall out** with stage players, whippe Kinge, **Queene,** magistrate, ladyes, and all that falles in his waye.

What **applicacion** doth hee **make of** the wordes in 822 page, where **hee saith** prophett Amos was forbidden to prophesie in the **Kinges Courte,** because hee **would** not have any sinne-rebuke-inge chaplaynes comme there, whoe knewe not howe to flatter, his mallyce is there **to** playne, and, as hee doth remember, the statute of 16 Hen. 8, cap. 16, sclaunderinge and diffameinge the Kinge is made **treason.** Yf Hen. 8 were alyve to rewarde him for this cen-**sure of** his expence in playes, and favoureinge them, hee should not **have the favour** to aunswere **it in this** Courte.

Mr. Pryn is not ignorante what emperour raigned when Ste **Peter and** Ste Paule preached obedyence, and surely, yf they held **it just, they** would as **well have** denounced vengeaunce against the **emperour as** against Ananias **and** Sapphira.

For his sentence, concurreth **with** my Lord Cottington; and that **some** publicque edicte bee made that all the bookes maye bee brought **in to** bee burnte.

Ep'us Cant.* Mr. Buckner, 100^{li} fyne, **and** imprysonmente accordinge to the course of **the** Courte.

For Sparckes, concurres **with my** Lorde Cottington.

For Mr. Pryn, he is sorrye that a man that hath been soe payn-**full and had** soe good breedinge should soe ill bestowe his labour **to such hayn**ous endes.

My Lord Cheiffe Justice **hath well tearmed** his booke, *Monstrum horrendum, informe, ingens,* **and might** verye well saie out the verse *(cui lumen ademptum),* for **there is** in it noe light of wisdome or understandinge.

It is a catholicque lybell, setteinge at defyaunce not onely the **Churche of** Rome, but the verye Catholicque Churche it selfe, and

* Archbishop Laud.

in a most infamous, daungerous, and treasonable waye, layeinge aspertion uppon the Kinge, Queene, magistrates, and all the kingdome; and to **wryte** any thing that maye have a treasonable exposicion is a most unexcuseable cryme, for hee that wryteth **cannott** tell of what disposicion his reader wilbee.

Butt he followeth the style of some of his predecessors of the same **secte, as Bukanan and Knottes**[a]**, whose doctryne was, that** it were **well there were a reward prefixt for those whoe kyll** tyrantes, as **there is for** those whoe kylles beares, wolves, and such thinges as destroye the comon wealth. And yf any Jesuite exceed this bloodye doctryne hee will forfeite his reputacion.

For his parte, hee doth hould playes in themselves tollerable, **yf** they **bee** voyde **of** obsceene and scurrilous passages, and that **there** is noe offence in them, the scurfe beinge taken awaye.

The reason whie playes have been universallye **dislyked is,** for that all **playes, before** Constantyne, were full **of** idolitarye, **and afterwarde lascivyous. And to** prove the vnlawfullnes of playes, Mr. Pryn **makes** some **52** sollogismes, whereof there is not one true. And one is, what has been condempned by 400 heathen philosophers, historians, poettes, &c., **must** necessarelye **be** condempned as unlawfull. Playes **have been soe** condempned, &c.: Ergo, they must bee unlawfull, **&c.**

By the **same reason hee maye** condempne Christian religion, **for** for that hath been condempned by **40** heathen philosophers, &c., and **alsoe by** the same reason, hee maye prove the world to bee **everlastinge,** for as manye philosophers, historians, &c. have maintayned that opinyon.

And that playes are in themselves indifferent it maye playnelye appeare **in that auncient devynes in** all ages have eyther allowed or have **been aucthours of** enterludes.

In the **lyfe time of Clemens** Alexandrinus, **which was 100 yeares** after Christe, one made **a playe** of Moses **his storye.**

[a] Knox.

In the **yeare 377** Ste Gregorye **Nazienzen** writt a **tragedye in** Greeke.

Rodulfus Gualter made another.

John Foxe, another called Christus Triumphans. Theodorus Beza made a **tragedye in** French, and Johannes Nichomedus translated it **into Latyn.**

Yea, George Bukanan made alsoe a tragedye of S^{te} Jo: Baptista, and surelye yf playes were *mala in se*, theis fathers would not have written them.

Hee is gladd that their lo^{pps} have alreadye soe **well** vindicated the wronges **the** Churche receyved by this man, concurres in his sentence with the highest, saveinge in the croppinge of his **eares.**

Lo. Tre'r.*   **Mr.** Pryn maketh himselfe **a** judge over the Kinge and **all** the **kingdome,** devideth his booke into severall actes, the sceene is the **world, but there** is but **one actour, and** hee plaieth the devill and the foole.

Playes were tollerated in all ages, and hee might have founde out some more worthie persons then Neroe, Caligula, Heliogabulus, to **compare with** his Matie, and not to compare the best of men to the worst of tyrantes. Yf there bee any faulte in the magistrates and governmente it is for sufferinge such as hee is.

Hee findes him a man of **noe partes,** patching papers **together,** every leffe full of falsitye and blunders, and thinckes **him to bee** lyke **the** miserable person in Seneca, whoe was soe deformed that noe mankinde could bee found in him. Agreeth with the highest.

For Mr. Buckner and **Mr.** Sparkes, with secretarye Windebancke.

* The Earl of Portland.

II.

PETITION OF WILLIAM PRYNNE, FEBRUARY, 1634.

[State Papers, Domestic, Charles I. cclx. 120.]

To the Right Honorable the Lords of his Majesty's Most Honorable Privie Councell. The humble petition of William Prynne, a prisoner in the Fleet,

Most humbly sheweth,

That your pore petitioner hath latelie incurred **your Lordships'** just and heavie censure for divers passages **inconsideratelie fallen** from his pen in a booke called Histrio-Mastix, which have given great and just offence to the King's most excellent Majesty, his royall Consort the Queen, and the whole state, the execution of which **sentence** will prove his utter overthrow and ruine, unles your Lordships wilbe graciouslie pleased to become his honorable intercessors to his Majesty for the mitigation **and remission thereof.**

He therefore in all humble submission prostrates himselfe **at your** Lordships' feet, professing his unfained sorrow for the said offensive passages, and acknowledging the justice **of your** Lordships' proceedings and severe sentence against **him** for the same; most humblie **beseeching your** Lordships **out of your abundant** compassions to **commiserate the distressed** forlorne **condicion of** your sorrowful suppliant; **and** to become his favorable mediators to his Majesty for the mitigation **and** pardon of his fine and corporall punishment, and he shall ever pray for your Lordships.

WILLIAM PRYNNE.

III.

SENTENCE OF THE UNIVERSITY OF OXFORD UPON WILLIAM PRYNNE.

[State Papers, Domestic, Charles I. cclxvi. 60.]

Convocatio habita 29° Aprilis **Anno** Domini 1634 cujus causa **erat** (sic enim præfabatur Vicecancellarius) ut egregius ille **Histriomastix** præli stupor et idolum vulgi Gulielmus Prinn **e Camera Stellata** justissimo fulmine percussus gradu academico **quem** infamavit exueretur; dum enim **non** tantum in fabulas sed **in** res **et personas** sacras, in **candidissimos Principum** mores, **in** bonos et **literatos pene** singulos **(tanquam mundus** totus ageret histrioniam) **iisdem furiis** debacchatus est, ipse **tandem** factus est fabula, cujus **Actus primus a** degradatione incipit infœliciorem postea habitura catastrophen, quænam **vere** nobis in piaculari hæc[a] victima mactanda partes relicta[a] **sint ex** decreto curiæ ad nos transmisso intelligetis.

Lecto decreto admonuit Vicecancellarius quantum honoratissi**morum** Procerum judicio deberet Academia quod solliciti ne filii dedecus in matrem redundaret, Artiumque tituli in communionem **infamiæ** traherentur, **prolem** degenerem, quam nemo lubens tolleret, prius abdicandam censuerint. Rogavit igitur an expungi vellent **infame nomen e** matricula, et quod solam[a] **in** absentem licuit virum musis amœnioribus bonisque omnibus infestum e musarum contubernio **grad**u omni spoliatum **et** eundem publico programmate deturbari cujus tenor **sequitur.** Cum Gulielmus Prinn olim hujus Academiæ alumnus, **jam vero** opprobrium, **in quodam** contra Histrionis[a] libello **(Theatri** flagellum tantum **præferente ut in**

[a] Sic.

solium securius inveheretur) multa in **Principem, populum, ecclesiam, curiam, licentia plus quam Seneca evomuerit, animosque** omnium quantum in **eo erat, procitando tantum non classicum** cecinerit, veras **etiam** tragœdias **si daretur** occasio **concitaturus; cumque** decretum **e Camera Stellata ad nos pervenerit** quo **perspectum habemus hoc illi impune non cessisse** sed inter alia **gravissima** censuræ stigmata, non ultimo **loco habitum** quod dignus **videretur ut** priusquam **aurium (sensorii** disciplinæ**) jacturam faceret, titulo et gradu Academico exueretur; Nos** Bryanus **Duppa** Academiæ Oxoniæ **Procancellarius totusque** Senatus Academicus tam **dignæ, ut par** est, Censuræ obsecundantes ne in gloriam **hoc** calumniæ nomen inter humaniores disciplinas audiatur, prodictum William Prinn e Studiosorum numero, ex quo **suis ipse** moribus sese jam antea expunxerat, publico prorsus scito **delemus et ne** Artibus ulterius inde honestamentum cedat infinum, illi quem hic exceperat gradem detrahimus, Ut Academia nostra cujus salutares succos in **venena mutavit tam** indigno nomine liberata eum posthac non agnoscat filium qui inpie adeo discessit in Reipublicæ ecclesiæ et bonorum omnium hostem.

Lecto Programmate plenis suffragiis amuit[a] Senatus Academicus sigillo publico muniri, jussit valvis etiam publicis appendi; **quæ** omnia expuncto **prius** nomine e matricula **peracta esse in perpetuam** rei memoriam **testantur** hæc acta publica.

[a] Sic for "annuit".

IV.

LETTER FROM WILLIAM PRYNNE TO ARCHBISHOP LAUD.[a]

[Add. MS. 5994, fol. 187.]

My Lord,

It is the *divyne asseveracion* of *the wisest of men, Ecclesiastes, vii. 7,* "Surely oppression maketh a wise man mad." Soe that I presume your Lordship will easily pardon me **if** the present pressures under which I languish cause me a little to forgett my self whiles I commemorate them unto you, not to mencion all or any of your *Lordship's private* verball *suggestions* against me to his Majesty (my most gracious soveraigne), which I hope I could with ease disprove upon an indifferent hearing; nor yet to recount those selected scatterd fragments or dimidiated sentences which *Dr.* *Heylin,* and *others your Lordship's charitable agents,* have concarcinated into one intire Informacion out of severall pages of my book in the method they were prosecuted at the hearing, annexing such horrid, seditious, disloyall, false glosses, applicacions, construccions, and inferences of theyr owne forging to them (contrary to the very letter, scope, and meaning of the passages themselves), as none but heads intoxicated with malice, disloyalty, and private revenge could ever fancye, wherewith *your Lordship* (if common fame speake truth) hath severall *tymes before* and since my censure

<small>Who *as himself reported was* specially *imployed by* your *Lordship to collect the severall passages in my booke that were offensive, that you might present them to his Majesty to incense* him the *more* against me.</small>

---

[a] From a copy in Dell's hand. The original was torn up by **Prynne** in the presence of Attorney-General **Heath.** The words in italics are underlined in the MS.

exasperated his Majesty *against me*. I shall onely **acquaint your Lordship** with some publicke passages of your episcopall **candor towardes me, both** in wordes and deeds, of which **the world takes too much notice, wherin** I doubt not but you will doe me **such right against yourself** as your Xtianity, place, and function joyntly **require, in case** I make it evident you have done me wronge, **anticipating the fruit of** all my petitions, **and** of the Queen's most gracious intercessions to his Majesty **for his most royall** grace and pardon, of which your *calumnyes and insolent solicitations have alone deprived me*. **To begin** with your verball injuryes, **which** in truth **are reall** wronges:—First, my Lord, you have **not onely** privately informed his Majesty and others, but publickely averred in the Starr Chamber, though extra-judicially before the **sentence**, that I have been ever factious and seditious since I **came into the world**; and that in the memory of man there never arose such a **pestilent, factious, seditious person,** both in Church and State, and **soe great an enemy to both, as I have been.** Certainly did your **Lordship know what a good** opinion the *whole* kingdome hath of your owne innocency in these particulars you object to me without proofe or truth, I suppose you would *have excepted yourself in this* hyperbolicall accusacion; **which as it displayed your** Lordship's archcharity and justice towardes me to the auditors, **what a true freind you** had been unto me, and what equity I might expect from **you in this** cause; for it seemed unto most who heard it a mere **malicious** slander, proceeding onely **from your** Lordship's over-**growne spleen, and derived to you** *by succession from Ananias* the **High** Preist, who by Tertullus his orator forged the very selfsame calumny **against innocent S.** Paule, Actes xxiv. 1. " Wee have found this man **a pestilent fellowe,** a mover of sedicion among the Jewes throughout **the** world, a ringleader of the sect of the Nazarens." For, my Lord, it is well knowne to many who then heard, and since have heard, of **this** your encomium, that I have ever from my cradle to this present demeaned my self religiously to my God, loyally to my soveraignes, dutifully to my superiors, lovingly to my

Exod. xxiii. 1; Psal. xv. 3.

Seditionis olim accusatus est etiam Christus, et omnes propemodum sancti viri et evangelici prædicatores. Pet. Martyr. Loc. Com. class 1, locus 30, sect. 1, 2. Solenne est ut Christianis nomina falsa sedicionis blasphemiæ et læsæ-Majestatis a persecutoribus affingantur, quibus tamen non sunt obnoxii. Centur. Magd. cent. 2, collat. 420.

equalls, curteously to my inferiors, inoffensively and **peaceably towardes** all men's persons, though I have oppugned **some men's** innovacions, superstitions, errors, **vices (the** onely faction **and sedicion of which I was** ever guilty, and of which your Lordship **can accuse me), and that** not out of any factious or seditious humour but to preserve the established receyved doctrines of our Church, and to doe the best good I could to the Church, the State, and soules of men. Yea I dare safely averr that there is noe man (how malicious soever) who **hath** knowne my life and conversacion but will acknowledge upon oath, if called to it (as three witnesses of creditt **examined by me** in this cause have done), that I have been **allwayes conformable to** the doctrine and discipline by lawe established in the **Church of** England (having kept and disswaded many from **inconformity** and schisme, of which the cruelty, insolency, violence, malice, pride, and such other vices of some prelats have been the **cheif occasions** for ought that I can fynde); that my life hath been **soe** innocent, blameles, peaceable, and free from faction or sedition, **as I was** never yet soe much as questioned or taxed for any the least misdemeanour or dissention during my four years' abode in the University of Oxford, or thirteen years' residence in Lincolnes Inne, where I prevented and composed sundry discordes, never **occasion**ing or fomenting any; nor having the least personall quarrell or **jarre with** any one member of those societies where I have lyved, but demeaning my self in such a manner as gained **me both** theyr **generall** respect and love, as they can joyntly testifye. All which **considered, I** hope your Lordship will doe me soe much justice as **to retract** this odious scandall (consisting onely **of** generalls, to **which noe** particular answere can be given) which I wish may not **truly reflect** upon your self, whiles you endeavour to fasten it upon **me, I trust** without a ground. Secondly, my Lord, **you have in** private suggested to his Majesty and others, and **openly affirmed in Starr** Chamber before the hearing, **that** my *Histriomastrix was compiled by combinacion;* that I had many handes and heads to assist **me** in it besides my owne, it being impossible for any man of what

---

"Peragit tranquilla potestas, quod violenta nequit mandataque fortius urget." Claudian. "Cruelty and violence have made many hereticques in all ages, but never reclaimed any."

profession soever, though sixty years old, to peruse or read **all those authorities quoted in it**. This, my **Lord**, I must profess **of my** owne certaine knowledge to be a notorious untruth, unbeseeming an Archbishop's sacred lippes, who should be ashamed **to be a** false accuser or slanderer of any man, especially in a publicke court of justice, as a judge, where nothing should be affirmed but what is undoubtedly true, and appear by proofes, confession, or certaine knowledge to be soe, neyther of which I am **sure** you had to justify this slander. Yea, you had my owne answere and examinacion upon oath, the written copye under my owne hand, and Mr. Atturney's **confession** in the informacion to ascertaine you that it was **compiled** by my **self alone, without** the helpe **or** assistance **of any other** whatsoever, which I challenge all the world to disprove. **Strange** therefore was it, that your Lordship, not onely without, but against such apparent evidence, should judicially publish **such a** falshod. And, wheras you then professed *you did vehemently suspect a party (and I heare you have nominated some particular man in private)* who had a hand in composing it, if your Lordship will be pleased to examine that party, or any other you suspect, upon oath, theyr very deposicions shall proclaime you a slanderer in this particular. Yea your owne severe censure of me, *your violent* **execucion of** my sentence upon me, even **to** the loss of my **eares and effusion of my** bloud (in which you alone would have noe voyce **in the** sentence, that soe you might have the onely hand, and be more singularly bloudy in the execucion, *which* **all wholly attribute** to *your despitefull malice to me and my profession*), as the onely **author** of the booke (which your selfe confessed to be lycensed, though you still prosecute me for it **with all** extremity—I say not to your shame), is an apparent proofe **that** you beleived me in your conscience **to be** the sole author **of it**, though you published the **contrary** with your mouth of purpose to defame me. Else why should I suffer soe much from you for it as **noe man ever yet** endured for an authorized booke of such a subject, **which noe Archbishop** ever yet *oppugned but your* selfe *who should* **have patronized it**. And wheras you

" Di-imini pastores cum altis raptores; paucos habemus. Pen past; res multos tamen excommuni a ores. Et utinam sufficeret votis lac et lana, sit tis enim sanguinem," &c. Bern. ad Clericum Serm

This is vox populi; how true it is your Grace may best determine.

affirmed that noe man of whatever profession could in **sixty years** space peruse those bookes I have **quoted** in it, therefore **I must** needs have the helpe of others; I here profess to your Lordship **that,** though I am not above thirty-three years old, yet I have perused all those bookes and quotacions with my owne eyes alone, and not taken them upon trust or relacion from others (*as your Lordship doth many things, and in particular your cavills* against some passages and sillogismes in my booke, which you **confessed** at the sentence you had noe *leysure to* **read***,* though tyme and conscience enough to censure, how justly you shall see anon), and not onely those, **but all such** I have **quoted in** my other treatises, with diverse **more authors in** my owne profession, in which I was noe ill proficient, **though** now deprived of it, yet never offending in it, a case seldome heard of untill now; and I doubt not but hundreds **in this** kingdome, not **many years** elder than my selfe, have read **more** authors then **I have cited,** though perchance your Lordship **and other** great prelats (whose many secular imployments, and it **may be** theyr *over laborious preaching once or twice a yeare, permit them not to read* or studye halfe soe much as meaner men) have not **perused or** read neare soe **many,** and therefore hate or envye such **as are more** studious or **industrious** then themselves; wheras they **should favour** and respect them most of any, giving **all** encouragements **to** promote theyr studyes **for** the publicke **good,** which oft tymes they most ungratefully reward with hatred **and** slanders, and a world of oppositions. **This second** slander therefore being **totally untrue,** if there **be any** equity or justice in **your** Lordship **I hope you** will recant it (and the precedent too), both to his Majesty **and** others who **have been** seduced by it, through your false informacions, to my irreparable prejudice and great inquietacion. Thirdly, my Lord, you have exceedingly injured **both your selfe and me, in** misreciting some arguments and wresting some passages **of my** booke in your very censure, which in justice **you** should have **read your** self before you did condemne them, and not trusted onely to Dr. Heylin's notes, **which** have deceived both your self and

---

It hath been ever a constant rule in Star Chamber in former times that noe man ought to be put from his profession (it being his freehold and livelyhood) unlesse he hath grievously offended **in** it, and that offence **to be** particularly charged **and** proved against **him. Yet I** without any such charge, offence, or proofe **at** all, must be debarred **and** put from my calling, that soe I may have nothing left me to subs'st **by,** which most men **thinke** hard justice, especially for a lycensed booke, compiled out **of counsells,** fathers, and **other** approved authors, **whose** wordes and opinions **I have** but transcribed.

others. The first sillogisme you were pleased to quarrell at was this. Page 9:

"That which had its birth and primary concepcion from the very devill himself (who is all and onely evill) must needs be sinfull, pernicious, unseemly, yea altogether unlawfull unto Xtians."

"But stage playes had theyr birth and primary concepcion from the very devill himself, who is all and onely evill." *Ergo*, &c. The minor you acknowledged for a truth fully manifested by the authors I there quoted, which made all the judicious auditors wonder to heare your Grace soe earnestly plead for stage playes, whose birth and originall you confessed to proceed from the very devill himself, and which the fathers with sundry others define to be the works and pompes of the devill wee all renounce in baptisme, which any Xtians and much more an Archprelate should be ashamed to plead for in a Court of Justice, *where none else argued for them but disclaimed theyr defence*. The onely thing you here excepted against was, not to the forme or substance of the major (which are undenyable if there be any logicke or truth in the fathers or *Scriptures* there quoted to confirme it, neyther did nor can you refell it), but onely to this parenthesis in it (who is all and onely evill), without which both the proposicion and sillogisme are compleat and firme, which you there affirmed to be both an absurdity, implying that all evill was inclusively in the devill, and soe none at all in man; and alsoe plaine manichisme, intimating the very entity of the devill to be evill, as he is a creature. But, had your Lordship been soe just as to knowe before you judged, you would have forborne this rash censure, since I thus explaine this very expression. Pages 14, 15 (which it seems you never read), "That the devill is all and onely evill," I mean in his quality as a devill, not in his entity as a creature, quoting this sentence of St. Ambrose in the margent, " Diaboli naturæ non improba, sed opera iniqua." And whether this be an absurdity or manichisme to stile the devill all and onely evill, that is onely evill in respect of his quality onely, and *quatenus* a devill, not of his entity as a creature (in which sense it is most true), I referr to all men's judgments and your Lordship's too, who must needs confess it an error in yourself, if not a slander, to impute that heresy to me in a publicke court of justice, as I thus *in terminis* denye. Which how great a sinne, a shame it is for an Archbishop a judge to doe in his very censure in such an high court in the audyence of soe great an assembly, and that upon a premeditacion too, your owne conscience (if it be not seared) must informe you, if not condemne you for it.

<small>Exod. xxiii. 1, 2 ; Psal. xv. 2, 3 ; Isa. v. 20 ; Psa. xciv. 20, 21, 23.</small>

The second syllogisme you undertooke to confute and shamefull misrecited was that of page 713.

That which forty heathen writers, philosophers, historians, orators, and poets of cheifest note have unanimously censured and condemned, from the very principles and remainders of corrupt nature, and theyr owne experimentall knowledge of its pernicious effects (all which you omitted), must doubtles be sinfull and alltogether abominable unto Xtians. Witness Rom. 2, 14, 15, to 29, Jer. 2, 10, 11, &c.

But these forty recited heathen writers, philosophers, historians, orators, and poets of cheifest note have unanimously censured and condemned stage playes from the very principles and remainders of corrupt nature, and theyr owne experimentall knowledge of theyr pernicious effects. *Ergo*, &c.

The minor you granted as true, whence diverse admired with what face your Lordship could justify stage playes in a court of publicke justice, when as you acknowledged that forty heathen authors of cheifest note had soe seriously condemned them as abominable and intolerable corrupcions, unless you meant to profess to all the world that you are more licentious and *farr worse than pagans*. The major you exceedingly triumphed over as a most absurd proposicion, when as I dare confidently affirme that noe Xtians nor pagan whatsoever, but onely a *professed Atheist*, can be *soe shameless to deny* it in that forme and with those limitacions as I propound it. But your Lordship looking upon it in hast, or with other men's eyes (and those perchance malicious), recited it but by fragments thus:—

"That which forty heathen philosophers, historians, orators, and poets, have unanimously condemned, must doubtless be unlawfull unto Xtians," omitting the limitacion which makes it every waye undenyable, (to witt from the very principles and remainders of corrupt nature and theyr owne experimentall knowledge of its pernicious effects). Which unfaithfull dealing how well it became your Lordship's rochet and justice in such a publicke place of judicature and such a judicious assembly let the world determine. This proposicion then which your Lordship soe learnedly, soe copiously refelled, was onely your owne, not myne, soe as you might have well spared all your paines to refute it. But, admit the major had been such as your Lordship fancyed, yet I say it is most true and undenyable in case of manners and abuses (and soe of stage playes to which I onely applye it), and in all divine truthes founded in the lawe of nature, of which heathen men by the light of nature are competent judges; witness, Acts 17, 27, 28, 29; Rom. 1, 20, 21; cap. 2, 14, 15; Jer. 2, 9, 10, cap. 18, 13, 14; 1 Cor. 5, 1, cap. 11, 14, 15; Tit. 1, 12, 13; Ezek. 16, 47 to 60; Prov. 24, 24; which conclude that there is a God, and He invisible, because heathen poets and Gentils acknowledge it, and that incest, lying, forsakeinge of God, injustice, flattery, and such like sinns are evill, because the very heathen themselves and theyr writers doe condemne them, which texts must be expugned out of the booke of God, and God himself taxed for an ill logician; if this proposicion you quarrell with be untrue, the commonest argument in all sortes of writers (especially in Chrysostome, Salvian, and other Xtian authors, who most sharply declaime against men's vices), and the frequentest medium in pulpits and all invectives against vices to manifest them to be evill; in shaking in censuring of which you shake and censure all these Scriptures, yea blame all Xtian writers and preachers for injudiciousnes, in pressing thinges to be evill, because pagans themselves detest and write against them; and wheras your Lordship learnedly objected that, if this medium were good, then it would followe that Xtian religion is ill because heathen writers condemne it, I answere, first, that noe such consequent can be inforced from it as I propound it, because they condemned religion not from the light of nature or theyr owne experimentall knowledge of its pernicious effects, but onely out of ignorance, the instigation of Satan, the pravity of theyr natures and antipathy to the truth. Secondly, your instances in Xtian religion and the Creacion are impertinent and fallacious, for, these being revealed truthes above the sphere of nature, heathen philosophers and others are not competent judges of them, because they are spiritually discerned, and apprehended onely by the eye of faith, 2 Cor. 2, 6, to 16, Hebr. 11, 3 ; wheras they are all able umpyres of all vices and vertues, of thinges that are morally good or evill, as the fore-quoted scriptures and all Xtian writers graunt, and soe of stage playes too. Soe that your owne indefinite proposicion is universally true in all poyntes of morality (in which sense I onely intended and applye it) though not in poyntes of supernaturall revealed truths, which were not in dispute; all which well weighed your Lordship had small reason to proclaime your selfe a conqueror in overthrowing both my syllogismes, before you had vanquished eyther of them, even as yourself propounded them; and truly, my Lord, had you seriously considered the weaknes of your owne two arguments to prove stage playes lawfull, you would have had little cause to except against my syllogismes to manifest them unlawfull. Your first argument, if reduced into forme, was thus:

Gregory Nazianzen (even then when himself and other fathers condemned stage playes, as directlye contrary to Xtian religion and good manners) wrote a tragedy called Christus patiens: ergo, common stage playes are commendable and lawfull in a Xtian state.

Had your Lordship concluded thus, Ergo, it is lawfull for common actors to play Xtians passion on the stage, the consequent had been more formall though farr more impious and unchristian then now, it being the very height of all impiety and prophanenesses to bring our Saviours *person or passion on the stage*, which not onely Protestants but even Popish counsells, writers, and our owne statutes have most severely censured as most abominable and prophane, though your Lordship (who taxed one for stiling it a Jesuiticall practise when as I might have added a diabolicall too) then seemed to approve it, or else this instance of Nazianzen's were improper. But this argument (as it was then propounded) hath noe coherence or solidity in it; for first the antecedent is false, that tragedy of Christus patiens which you soe confidently affirmed to be Nazianzen's being none of his, but a mere spurious bratt, though printed with his workes, as both Baronius, Bellarmine, Lewenclavius, Possevine, with other learned Papists, and Mr. Cooke in his Censura, p. 125, with other Protestants, joyntly testify, and I have proved in my Histriomastix, p. 833, 834, 835, where you might have read a satisfactory answere to this and your following arguments; I wonder therfor your Lordship should soe farr forgett yourselfe, even in poynt of schollership, as to affirme this tragedy to be his, when all learned men affirme the contrary, an oversight not pardonable in your Lordship at such a tyme and place of expectacion. Secondly, admit it is, yet what consequence is this? Nazianzen penned a poeme of Christ's passion onely to be read, which to act were most prophane; ergo, it is lawfull and commendable to act common stage playes. Certainly graunt every action, and this act of Nazianzen lawfull (which is not a thinge soe de fide, though your Lordship lay it downe as a positive ground, but that it may be safely denyed); yet this argument is so illogicall (though your Lordship's best to prove stage playes lawfull) that a puniest sophister would deride it, as I have largely proved in my booke, which might have rectifyed this your gross mistake had you been pleased to read it ere you censured it. Your Lordship's second argument for playes was this: Buchanan compiled a tragedy of Jeptha's daughter; Beza himself a tragedy called Abrahamus Sacrificans; a late Lutheran hath turned some other Scripture storyes into tragedyes; ergo, common stage playes are lawfull and tollerable in a Xtian Republike.

Had your Lordship concluded properly, ergo, it is lawfull for common players to act sacred Scripture storeys on the stage, as the antecedent seems to imply, the whole auditory then present would have cryed shame upon you, since our owne statutes, with sundry counsells and authors quoted in my booke, condemne this impious practise as most execrably prophane. However, the argument itself (which I have there largely answered) is but a mere inconsequent, these tragedyes being penned onely to be read, not acted, as I have proved, p. 833, 834, 835, and elswhere. And whatever Buchanan and Beza wrote (the sole medium to make good your argument), being not soe authentique as to pass for current truth, since they wrote against bishopps and some ceremonyes of our Church, which I presume your Lordship dares not conclude to be unlawfull because they writt against them, though you argue stage playes to be lawfull for this reason, onely because they penned these two tragedyes; a very sandy foundacion, on which I thought noe bishopps would or could have built unless those authors had been more freindly to them. And here, my Lord, to paye you with your owne coyne, give me leave to inform you thus much, that in both these arguments you use that very medium or substance as irrefragable which you censured as absurd and false in me. I concluded stage playes unlawfull because forty heathen writers (even from the principles of corrupt nature and the experyence of theyr lewdnes) had condemned them; which you, misreciting, endeavoured to prove absurd, and yet you argue stage playes to be lawfull onely because Nazianzen, Buchanan, Beza, and a Lutheran had penned four sacred tragedyes. A medium of the selfe same nature, and not soe authentique as myne, since forty are more likely to be orthodox then four, and that which is condemned by the principles of nature and experyence of its illnes is more probable to be ill then that which those four did (perchance in theyr younger dayes), without any divyne precept or example, is likely to be good. Your Lordship therefore might have in charity forborne to quarrell with my two syllogismes against stage playes (which are both formall and substantiall too) till you had produced some better of your owne in theyr defence; these two being neyther formall nor substantiall,

all together unworthy your Lordship's place and learning, or that judicious court or auditory for whose satisfaccion you were pleased to propound them. From your excepcions against my sillogismes I shall proceed to some passages in the book which your Lordship proclaimed to implye the lawfulnes of subjects laying violent handes upon the sacred persons of princes, and to be noe less then high treason, of both which I hope your Lordship will pronounce me innocent when you have heard my answere, though I have allready suffered for them as a nocent. The maine passages upon which you grounded this accusacion were those of fol. 555: "These Emperors' stage delights being the just occasions of theyr untimely deaths." And p. 489: "An end most suitable to his vitious, tyrannical, and play-adoring life." Written of Caligula slayne by Chermea. But under your Lordship's favour I conceyve that neyther of these two passages are treason or sedetion, or any tacit approbacion of this disloyall assertion, as I use them: not treason, because not within the statute of 25 Ed. III. c. 2, nor any wayes reflecting upon his Majestyes or his royall Consort's persons, being applyed to other purposes and transcribed out of other approved authors: not seditious, intimating the lawfulnes of murdering princes in some cases; for first, this phrase (just occasion) can have noe such implicacion as I there use it; first, because I stile these Emperors' stage-delights the just occasions of theyr untimely deaths in respect of God's avenging justice onely, who sometimes takes occasion for small offences to punish wicked men, not onely with eternall, but even with temporall, death; the wages due to every sinne, if God please in justice to render it, in this sense alone is evident by the whole scene, wherein it is being nothing else but a particular commemoracion of God's just judgments upon play-poets, players, and playhaunters, whose deaths, as I there stile just judgments of God, soe I phrase those stage delights which occasioned them just occasions with reference onely to God's just judgments, as the whole context and the intencion of it manifest, both which may be truly called just in regard of God in a good and proper

Indeed Dr. Heylin, imployed by your Lordship to peruse my booke, reported to diverse that he had found high treason in it (perhaps against his S. George), meaning those two passages, and that he hoped he should have my life and head for it, though himself be guilty of the self-same treason, and worse, in his Geography, and S. George, as I could easily prove. And his learned judgment perchance directed your Lordship's verdict to finde and stile these passages treason.

sense (as Mr. **Atturney** himself acknowledged), and **yet** theyr murders be most impious in respect of **those which** slew them; as was our Saviour's death, most **just and** justly **occasioned** in regard **of God, as a** surety for our sinnes, yet most unjust and sinfull **in respect of** Pilat, Judas, and **the** Jews. Math. 21, 3, 4, 18 to 26; Acts 2, 23, c. 4, 27, 28; Isay. 53, 4 to 12. Secondly, because **I call** these theyr **untimely** deaths (not execucion, as was pretended, but) murder, treason, **and conspiracye,** in reference to those who slew them (fol. **555, p. 118, 465, 799, 826,** 849), the very greatest brandes of dislike, **of unlawfulnes, that I** could cast upon them. This phrase therfore **of** just **occasion can** never imply theyr murders lawfull unless you will proclaime murder, treason, and conspiracy lawfull, which were **a** contradiction. Thirdly, because **I** in terminis condemne this very posicion of murdering princes, for faction and rebellion, and the practise of it for treason, p. 826, and **796, 823 to 828,** quoting such **scripture** and English writers against me, **in the** margent, as **doe most** solidly displaye and refute it. **What therfore I** thus **professedly condemne,** malice it self cannot justly affirme. **I** tacitly **implye, since expressum** facit cessare tacitum, as all lawes accord. **Fourthly, because** I condemne all murders in **generall,** upon any **pretended** good, or publike end whatsoever, **p. 943,** 182, f. 519; **all** murders at stage playes in speciall, and stage **players** themselves **as the** occasions of murders, fol. 516 to 520. **Therfore I** must necessarily **condemne those** Emperors' murders **occasioned** by stage **playes,** and committed **at** them, it being a **direct** contradiction **to** conceyve those murders at or occasioned by stage **playes** lawfull, **when as** I condemne **all** murders at them or caused **by** them as unlawfull, and censure playes themselves as the occasions **of** them. **Fifthly,** because I directly averr in my answere upon **oath** that I doe **and did** ever detest and renounce this doctrine of the lawfulnes of **subjects** laying violent hands upon the sacred persons **of** princes for any cause whatsoever, as wicked, hereticall, **and** disloyall, contrary to the very oath of allegiance which I had **thrice** taken to the lawes and statutes **of** our realme and doctrine of our Church, which must severely censure it; and what I thus expressly disclaime upon my oath noe lawe, noe charity, can presume me to approve upon a bare surmised implicacion from those two phrases, which doe not necessarily implye it, as Mr. Atturney himself acknowledged. The rather because I was never soe much as once suspected to be of this opinion, nor taxed of the least disloyalty to my Soveraigne; neyther doe eyther of these two expressions, or the places where they are cited, tend to justify or insinuate any such doctrine. And wheras your Lordship was pleased to reply in your sentence that I condemne this assertion in my book and answere, as the doctrine of popish priests and Jesuits onely, but yet insinuate and approve it as the doctrine of the Puritans, whom ye endeavoured to prove farr worse than any priests or Jesuites (*who are much beholding to you for your good opinion of them*) by a discourse stollen almost verbatim out of *Barford the Jesuite's answere* to Deus and Rex, where all the Puritan authors you then quoted are recited (the very worst of all which you then confessed to be Ponet, Bishop of Winchester, one of your owne rochet, and a bishop Puritan, if a Puritan). My Lord, I would have you knowe that as I detest this doctrine as jesuiticall soe I abhorre all jesuiticall equivocations too (in which your Lordship, perchance, is too well versed), and yet I absolutely condemne this doctrine in all respects by whomsoever justified; the very wordes of my answere being, that the popish priests' and Jesuites' doctrine, *and the doctryne of all others*, of the lawfulnes of destroying princes (which I doe and did allwayes detest from my heart as impious, hereticall, and abominable, &c.), is noe other than faction and rebellion; and the practise of it treason, murder, and conspiracy, a direct falsificacion of your Lordship's forged replye. Sixthly, admit I had stiled them just occasions in regard of the Emperors themselves, or those who slew them as you pretended, yet it follows not therupon that theyr murders were just and lawfull. David's adultery was a just, a great occasion for the enemyes of God to blaspheme, 2 Sam. 12, 14, yet theyr blasphemy though thus justly occasioned was a sinne. The Jewes' ill lives were a just occasion for the Gentils

[Indeed bishops have been guilty of soe many treasons in doctrine and practise in former tymes here in England that one had written a particular treatise, de proditionibus Prælatorum et conquestu; though I never found any treatise de proditionibus Puritanorum.]

to blaspheme the name of God, Rom. 2, 24, yet the Gentills' blasphemy was unlawfull. One Xtian may give a just occasion of scandall to another, yet it may be a sinne in him to be scandalized at it. Rom. 14, 13, 15. One man by his reproachfull speeches or actions may give just occasion (the commonest expression wee use in all such cases) to another to revile or strike him, a case which every day falls out, yet his reviling or striking of him [a] for such an indignity noe legall or just waye of punishment, Rom. 12, 17, 19, 20. One man assaults another with a resolucion to kill him in such a place and manner as he must eyther kill or be killed, wherupon he killes the assailant in defence of his owne life. All men in such cases graunt that the assailant gave the defendant just occasion to slay him, yet his killing of him is unlawfull and manslaughter by our lawe, for which he shall be arraigned and loose his goodes, and life too in case he cannot read. By all which instances (and hundred others of this nature) it is evident, that, though I stile the occasions of those Emperors' murders just in respect of those who slew them (in which sense I never meant it, but in reference to God alone), yet it follows not thereupon that theyr murders were just; since the occasion may be just, yet the consequent, the manner of murdering them, unjust in those who did it, as all those parallel examples evidence. Lastly, this phrase of just occasions is common in many authors, and in most men's mouths especially upon injuryes or discurtesyes receyved; yet none ever tooke such offence, or made such construccion of it in others, as your Lordship hath made of it in my case. Yea, though Mr. Atturney confessed it might have a good interpretacion in this very place with reference unto God alone, and that schollers who understood distinctions would take it in this sense, but the ignorant vulgar might be seduced by it, yet this would not move your Lordship (though lawe and equity doe ever enjoyne the most favourable construction to be made in all courts of justice), being a scholler, yea, a father by place and profession in our Church (who should be

[side note: See S. Pet. writes, 2 Pet. 3, 16. That the unlearned and unstable wrest S. Paul's Epistles and the other Scriptures to theyr owne destruccion. Yes, the Jesuites and others wrest them to the destruccion of princes. Shall wee therfore condemne and burne the Scriptures as seditious and dangerous]

[side note: [are unlawfull. 1 Pet. 3. And that not in point of conscience but of law, he being noe meet judge to avenge or right himself and his reviling or striking him;]]

[a] The words in brackets are in the margin in the original, having been omitted by Dell in copying.

full of charity), to conster it in that fayre **inoffensive sense** in writings because they are thus abured? Yet my **which** I onely meant it, as the premises evydence; **not in that** booke must suffer because some ignorants may misuncharitable, seditious, disloyall, wrested sense alone, **for which** conster or misapply this phrase of just occasions there is (as I conceyve) noe ground or shadowe as the premised and the insuing passages contrary to theyr sense reasons infallibly demonstrated; and as this phrase (just occasions) and myne. warrants noe such siditious inference as your Lordship pretended, soe **neyther doth** that other expression, "And end most sutable to his vitious, tyrannicall, play-adoreing life." Which, as it implyes his untimely death to be ill (not just **or lawfull) because his** life was such, and yet it was sutable to his life in regard of God's justice onely, which suffers wicked men to come to evill endes, soe it is **the very** expression of Grimston in his Imperiall History, printed **and published** by authority, 1623, pages 160, 250. Who both **there and in** pages 104, 147, 156, 180, 184, 194, 222, 246, 52, 552, writes **thus of** Caligula, Domitian, Heliogabalus, Gallienus, Valentinian, **and other** Emperors' murders and untimely deathes. **They** dyed according to **theyr** defects, and conformable to their lives they had lyved; for it is the will of God that wicked princes make evill endes. They had such a death as theyr filthy life deserved. They were slayne and poysoned by God's just judgment **and as** they deserved, &c.; which very expressions are contained in Speed's Chronicle, page 445; in Howe's Chronicle, dedicated to his Majesty, 1631, pages 119, 325; in Dr. Beard's Theatre of God's Judgments, edit. 4. 1631, pages 42, 43, 117, **134,** 180, 181, 290, 331, 337, **493, 546,** 558; in Sir Walter **Raleigh's** History of the World and the preface to it; in Raynolds, his treatise of M   , and in all authors who have written of God's judgments, or collected any examples of his justice upon sinners. These have ever passed free from all excepcions or the least suspition of any such seditious insinuacion as your Lordship hath inferred from them in my booke. You must now eyther make all authors who use these or such like phrases guilty of treason, sedition, or this pretended doctrine of murdering princes, as well as I, or else acquit me of it in excusing them; the rather because I have answered on my oath **that** I had noe such disloyall intention **in all or** any of those

expressions as your Lordship censured me for, from these very
phrases onely without any other proofes. Soe superabundant hath
your Lordship's charity towardes me been as thus to **interpret** my
meaning quite contrary to my oath, intencion, scope, words, and
the usuall acceptacion of those very phrases in all other authors, **of
purpose to make me** guilty of sedicion and disloyalty by mere
implications, and wrested inferences, of which my heart was never
conscious, neyther doe my wordes implye; and is this your Lordship's arch-charity, piety, clemencye, or justice to racke your wittes,
your power, my wordes **and meaning, thus to make me** culpable
and disloyall where my heart, my expressions too (at least **in** my
intention, opinion, and vulgar acceptacion), are innocent and sincere?
Would your Lordship be well pleased to have been dealt with thus
by others as you have dealt with me in these particulars and in the
whole prosecution of this cause? Alas, what author shall be innocent in judgment; whose life, whose liberty, or estate exempt from
danger **every** hower, if neyther his oath, his owne express determi-
nacion, his innocency of conversacion, the publike allowance, entry,
or lawful printing and publishing of his booke by those whom the
state appoyntes, the common acceptacion of his expressions in all
other authors, nor his very scope and intencion (the best inter-
preters of his meaning) can acquit him from such a seditious, harsh,
strained interpretacion of his wordes, as never **soe much as entered
his** heart **to** conceyve: every of which **in former ages and** cases
have been sufficyent **to clear** poore accused innocents; yet all of
them combined together **have** yeelded **noe** such priviledge to me,
or those objected passages; who have **been not** onely censured
but executed *by your Lordship as seditious* and disloyall, though I
trust it now most **evidently appears unto** you (as it doth to most
men else who have **eyther heard or read** them or knowne me) that
neyther they nor I are such? As your Lordship hath misused
those two passages, soe have you dealt with that of page 321: "Not
to mencion the over prodigall disbursments upon playes and maskes
of late penurious tymes which have been well nigh as expensive as

the warrs, and more chargeable to many then theyr **soules**," &c. (recited onely by peece-meale, by which fayre kynde of **dealing** the most innocent passages may be made offensive); which, **though** I intended merely of the over prodigall expenses of our ordinary play-haunters upon common playes and **maskes** in our publike theatres (as the whole scene and subsequent wordes demonstrate), at which our playhaunters annually **spend** as much well nigh as is **or hath been** yearly contributed to or spent upon the warres, or **given by them** to ministers to instruct theyr soules (the cleare and onely scope and meaning of this passage), yet your Lordship **was** pleased to conster it a great intollerable scandall, both to his Majesty and the tymes, implying that his Majesty had spent **the sub**sidyes given him by Parliament to mainteyne the **warres upon** playes and maskes, and that our present tymes were **beggerly and** base. When as his Majesty (whom I never mencion **but with all**[a] honorable and dutifull expressions, stiling **him our** most gracious **soveraigne** lord, and his lawes most pious lawes, p. 715, 500, and **in** the table, the onely places where I name him) is neyther named, intimated, or intended in this passage, neyther can it be applyed to **him, since it** speakes onely of the expenses of common playhaunters at publike playes and theatres, as the **whole scene, the con**text, and last clause here recited (omitted in the reading evidence). Neyther are the present tymes soe much as named in it, but onely late penurious tymes indefinitely, by which I meant those two late years of scarcity, plague, and famine, wherein I penned this passage; **which his** Majesty by his proclamacions and orders to the **justices to cease the dearth,** together with the cryes of poore men, then **wanting both bread** and worke in many places, and **every** man's experience proclaimed to be penurious tymes in regard to the present dearth, **the scarcity** of corne and worke. Wherefore it could be noe scandall or **offence in me to stile those** tymes penurious in that sense, as all men **then and since have called them.** It hath **been a** receyved maxime in divinity, **lawe, and** conscience, that dubious wordes, which may have a good and bad interpretacion,

[a] To whom I dedicated my booke intituled Health's Sickness, and whom I have ever honoured and obeyed as my most gracious soveraigne.

ought ever to be construed in the most favourable and benigne sense in courtes of judicature, that the hardest sense which may expose the party to censure ought ever to be rejected, and that none ought to be censured for other men's inferences (for who then could be secure against malignant misconstruccions) but for his owne express posicions and wordes. Had this rule taken place in your Lordship's censure of the three preceding passages (upon which alone you grounded your sentence, as I and others apprehended) I doubt not but you had absolved me and them, whereas you passed sentence against us. But your Lordship hath been soe charitable in your construccion of all those passages (to omitt the other in my Perpetuity,[a] brought in by head and shoulders for want of other matter, which booke you burnt in private, without any sentence past against it) as to invert this rule to make me lyable to the severest censures the high court of justice could impose or thinke of. Which censures though they have been allready inflicted and for the *most part fully executed upon me by procuring*, yet as if they were farr too little, and I had not sufferd enough as yet for a licensed booke (the very subject whereof as was then confessed was not offensive but the stile alone), or for other men's false applicacions and misconstructions of my wordes, *you still proceed to exasperate his Majesty against me, to drawe me to a second censure and tribunall (where you are and shall be, as most suspect you have been hitherto, both my chief accuser, prosecutour, and judge) for the self same booke.* Alas, my Lord, is this your piety, charity, pitty, grace, or justice, to delight in men's perpetuall vexacion, for theyr very paines and *industry to advance the publike good*, and suppress those common abuses which all ages, all places, have constantly decryed, and our owne lawes condemned, or thus to racke theyr well meaning wordes, contrary to theyr express intended sense and scope, to make them scandalous and offensive by strained inferences, when in themselves they are not soe? Did ever our Savior, or any Apostle or saint of his, teach you such a lesson, or leave you such a

Sidenotes:
Soe are the express statutes of 26 Hen. VIII. c. 13; 1 Ed. VI. c. 12; 5 Ed. VI. c. 11; 1 Eliz. c. 6; 13 Eliz. c. 1; 14 Eliz. c. 1, 2, and other statutes.

Yet the fryers late booke of Deus Natura and Gratia, &c., to reconcile us to Rome and other such Popish pamphlets can be published, sold and printed without controll or question.

The statute of 1 Car. c. 1, to which your Lordship consented, thrice together called stage playes unlawfull pastimes.

---

[a] Prynne's first book, *The perpetuity of the regenerate man's estate*.

president?[a] Nay, he commandes you to be mercifull, **as your** heavenly father is mercifull, Luc. 6, 36, yet you *(as your actions* towardes me proclaime unto the world) delight in *nothing soe* **much** *as in being more cruell, merciless, oppressive, and vexatious* **then** *any other,* and *in shewing noe pitty at all.* He exhortes you to be meeke and lowly of heart as he was, Mat 11, 29, *and you are noted of most men to be of an exceeding fiery, insolent, virulent, implacable, malicious, and revengefull spirit in all your proceedings; verifying the old proverb, Asperius humili nihil est cum* **surgit** *in altum.* He enjoynes you to put on bowells of mercyes, kindnes, humblenes of mynde, meeknes and long suffering, forbearing **and** forgiving **others, even as Xt** forgave you, Col. 3, 12, 13. And you, in many men's judgment, have *quite unbowelled yourself of all mercyes, kyndnes, humblenes, meeknes,* and *long suffering,* **forbearing** *and forgiving none* whom you are able to crush *and ruyne, being soe brimfull* of enmity and malignity towards me (that I speake not of others), even for that wherein most expected. I should have had your best proteccion and encouragement the better to suppress those vicious abuses, which your dignity and function engage you to oppugne more then any; **that** though you have allready ruyned me in my body, profession, liberty, state, and reputacion, by expelling me the University of Oxford, and degrading **me there in the most** disgracefull manner, allbeit I never **offended in it,** *exiling me Lincolnes Inne, and thrusting me from my practise of the lawe, though I was never a delinquent in eyther,* fining me 500.0[l], a summe **infinitely** beyond my estate, causing me to stand upon two severall pilloryes, and there to loose both my cares, a punishment seldome or **never** inflicted upon any gent, graduat, or barrister, unless for such offences as the statutes of the realme expressly mulct with such a penalty), martyring my bookes before my face **in the most** despitefull manner, shutting me up fast in prison, both before and since my censure, tossing **me to and fro** from prison to prison, for greater vexacion and expence. **And all** this for the foremencioned misconstrued passages, perused and lycensed in a due accustomed

"Peccat ante in Deum quicunque episcopus qui non quasi conservat servis ministrat sed quasi Dominus; frequenter autem et quasi amarus Dominus, per vim similis constituitus Ægyptiis qui affligebant vitam filiorum Israel." Orig. Hom. 31, in Matth.

Multi cum Regiminis jura suscipiunt ad lacerandos subditos inardescunt. Terrorem potestatis exhibent et quibus prodesse debuerant nocent. Et quia charitatis visura non habent Domini videri appetunt. Patres se esse minimi recognoscunt humilitatis locum in elationis dominacionem immutant. Et si quando extrinsecus claudiantur intrinsecus sæviunt. De quibus veritas dicit venlunt ad nos in vestimentis ovium intus autem sunt lupi rapaces." Greg. Mag. Hom. 17, in Evangelia.

[a] i. e. "precedent."

manner, both in the written and printed copye (lycensed May 31, 1630, entered into the booke of **licenses,** under the **warden** of stacioners, the lycenser's, clarke of the stacioners handes, Octob. 16, 1630, finished at the press above **x.** weekes, and by the lycenser's owne appointment published in the countrey above **four** weekes before her Majesty's **pastorall,** against which it could not possibly be intended, as your Lordship and others surmised, being soe longe written, lycensed, and **printed before** it), yet your malice and enmity against me are still implacable, and **all** this I have undergone is too to little in your Lordship's most charitable opinion for such haynous lycensed offences. You will yet have a second encounter *with me, begging **of his** Majesty and the Star Chamber a further suite against me in the High Commission (which* I prayse God **I feare not)** that soe your Grace and the Church may disgorge and powre out the full and furious violls of your outragious wrath and vengeance on me, *as the state (I say not by your Lordship's sole instigacion) hath done.* That soe I may have noe being, noe rest or **peace** in eyther, and may (if possible) be sent suddenly packing **quick** to hell, for *wounding the Church and clergye in theyr beloved vices and corrupcions* (though with theyr owne authorized canons **and** writings onely), which are growne now soe delicate, soe arrogant, that they must not be touched, noe not to worke **theyr cure.** Which strange unparalleled violence and vexacion **of your** Grace *makes the world beleyve* (how truly I cannot, yourself upon serious **examinacion** of your owne hart and wayes may well determyne), *that you are wholly composed of rancor, malice, oppression, vexacion, cruelty, implacablenes, mischeif, and revengefull spleen, having noe bowells of compassion,* Xtianity, *charity, humanity, gene-*

^A Videtur omissum towards
them aut aliquid simile.

rosity, or goodnes in you, A *which are allwayes* pitteful, courteous, compassionate, mild, and just, abhoring all vexatious extremityes, especially towardes such who have been innocent, pious, and in**dustrious** in theyr courses. Truly, my Lord, did you but seriously consider with your self that you have been advanced (*allmost from the very dunghill*) to that transcendent place of honour and power **wherein** now you **are** seated only by his Majesty's most gracious favour, and that you now stand, and are, and have been supported by it alone, without which you might have been longe ere this (*and who knowes how soone you may be yet*) *a more contemptible spectacle of misery and justice* then myself; methinkes it should make you **more** moderate, just, and compassionate towardes others, since you need soe much compassion, pardon, and proteccion from others, *without which you could not long subsist in that state wherein you are*. I doubt not but you know that as you have some faultes and oversights, soe you have enemyes enough *allready* (*I will not say farr more then other man or prelate*) who would rejoyce to see your fall, your ruyne (which nothing will sooner procure then your false, scandalous accusacions, and violent vexatious proceedings, *both in Church and State, which all men generally detest and grone under*), and will you yet every *day* raise up more enemyes (yea more cryes and teares to *God*) against you by your illegall *exorbitant vexacions*, which **make** you *the* **common** odium of the **world** and *times*? Certainly he who makes *noe better* use of his **soveraignes superlative grace**, but valere ad *nocendum*, immoderately to vexe, oppress, undoe, and injure others, *to purchase* all men's hatred noe man's love, is unworthy such a *blessing, and cannot longe enjoye himself or it*. The philosophers could say, Nullum violentum est duiturnum; and the poet, Immodicis brevis est ætas, ac rara senectus. Yea, God himself hath positively resolved, Psal. 140, 11, " Evill shall hunt the violent man to overthrow him. His mischeif shall **returne** upon his owne pate, and his violent deeling shall come **downe** upon his owne head." Psal. 7, 16. And therefore lest self love instruct your Lordship to be more just and moderate, less violent and vexatious in your proceedings, to take heed of vexing or trampling downe others (especially innocents) without just cause, or by illegall means, for feare God and others, even in justice, tread downe you. *My Lord, you have been observed of late to grow more strangely violent and exorbitant every daye*, **and *I*** *have cause to beleive it. Every* man supposed that the **loss of** my **eares** and effusion of my bloud would have quenched (at least allayed) the furye **of your rage against** me. Yet, whiles my wounds were bleeding

---

" Nescio an nemo ad dandam veniam difficilior sit sæpius meruit." Senec. de Clementia, l. 1, cap. 6. Which booke and theme your Lordship maye doe well to studye.

Eccles. 4, 1; Exod. 2, 23. 29. Prelati pulvinos his exhibent a quibus se noceri posse in studio gloriæ temporalis timent. Quos vero contra se nil valere couspiciunt hos nimirum asperitate rigidæ semper invectionis premunt, nunquam clementer admonent sed pastoralis mansuetudinis obliti jure dominacionis terrent. Jactanter erga subditos se erigunt nec quid agere debeant sed quid valeant attendunt. Libet ut licenter illicita faciant et subditorum nemo contradicat. Quos recte per prophetam divina vox increpat dicens, vos antem cum austeritate imperabatis iis et cum potentia." Grego. Mag. Past. part 2. cap 8.

(oh! the abundant compassion and relentancye, or rather barbarous inhumane mercilesnes, of your obdurate heart) *you **caused**[a] Cross the pursevant*, in a strange, *illegall, unheard* of waye, ***by your mere verball command***, without *showing any* warrant, to seize upon my bookes, to carry them to his *house and there* to prayse if not to sell them, against all lawe, all *justice, without any* legall ground, there being yet noe extent *against me for* my fyne, and your Lordship having noe authority by lawe *to graunt it* after, much less before, the fyne estreated; which notable act of your Lordship's new justice and oppression (of one soe much afflicted by you before) in the middest of my corporall sufferings, makes many suspect **the equity** of your former proceedings, and to divyne what justice I must looke for at your hands in the High Commission, since you thus unjustly seise upon my bookes, the onely instruments to justify and defend my cause against your proceedings there; it being the **very extremity** of injustice thus illegally to disarm me of the means of my just defence, and then to proceed against me. Had my fyne been estreated, and the sheriff by a legall process extended my bookes, there had been some coulor of justice in it (though it hath been reputed lawe in former tymes that a scholler could not **be** distrained by his bookes noe more then a smith by his anvill or an husbandman by his plowe, because they are the necessary instru**ments of his** profession); or had not Sir William Beecher and Mr. Atturney severally surveyed my studye by order from your Lordship and other the Lords of his Majesty's Privy Counsell, and after by theyr direccion restored those bookes unto me (which they neyther would nor could detayne from me in justice after these surveys, they being my proper goods), your Lordship might have had some seeming pretence to seise them (though I knowe no lawe or precedent for it), to see whether there were any unlawfull bookes amonge them; but to doe it before my fyne estreated, **and that by** a pursevant, not a sheriff or his bayly, without any legall process, by your owne immediate authority, after two surveyes and restitucion of them to me by order, and that not to peruse but to prayse

---

[a] Laud denied having given the order.

and *sell them, of purpose (as some conjecture)* **to** *anticipate* **my**
defence in the High Commission, is such a transcendent straine **of**
oppression and injustice as all men wonder at and exclaime **against.**
Some saye *(I made Will Lau) is your Lordship's anagram*,[a] **who** Yet God enjoynes Bishops
oft tymes make your will (not lawe or canons) the onely rule of not to be self willed nor
many **actions. I am sure of** this **your** seizure, in which your soone angry. Tit. 1. 7.
anagram is truly verifyed. *And how extravagantly unjust that* man
must be in all *his courses who makes his will his onely lawe* (as if
he had noe God, *noe Scripture, noe conscience, noe reason*, noe justice, noe *humane lawes to bound, direct, or oversway him*), how pre-
cipitately he must post on to temporall and eternall ruyne, all
moderate upright men may easily discerne. Wherfore, my **Lord**,
though you are great be you not unjust; *though you thinke yourself
above the lawes eyther of God or man*, yet be not **lawless in** your
actions; though you are powerfull, yet be not vexatious, malicious,
and despitefull, to[b] remember that for all **your** power **and favour**
you are but dust and ashes, **a man and** not a god, a subject not a
soveraigne, and therefore doe to others as you would have them doe
to you were you in theyr condicion, and they in yours. And
knowe withall if you will still proceed to prosecute, to oppress an
innocent with violence and vexacion, that there is one **in heaven**
and another in earth above you, to whom I shall appeale for justice
in case you refuse **to doe me voluntary** *right against yourself, in all
the premised particulars of your* injustice towardes me; of which
perchance you have been ignorant, or altogether senseless heretofore,
but **cannot be** misconusant **or** regardless **now,** after soe large a
private discovery and relation of them to yourselfe, which I had
never made had not I found your spleen against me restless, end-
less, without all boundes or reason; in which involuntary relacion,
if I have manifested **more** distemper, choler, or dealt more plainly,
more uncomely with your Lordship then beseems me, I hope you
will consider that *lasa patientia fit furor*, **and that your violence,**

[a] For " William Laud." [b] Sic in orig.

your injustice, have given me just occasion **a little to** forgett myself, whiles I thus privately sent my **manifold greivances and** pressures *to your* **Lordship,** *from whom they originally springe.* Neither can I doubt **your** Lordship's pardon for such *distempered oversights, who are* **every day farr** *more subject to them yourselfe.* All I requyre of your **Lordship is,** but to doe **me right** for all the forenamed *injuryes, in the self same waye* **and manner** *as you have wronged me, and to the self same persons, and to make such restitucion* to me both of my profession, liberty, goodes, and **good name** which you have taken from me, as may prepare **you to** receyve **remission** at the **handes of God,** upon your true repentance. Non remittititur peccatum nisi restituatur ablatum, **is a receyved canon** among all **casuists and** divynes. *If therefore you expect forgivenes at God's handes or myne, pray make me now such voluntary, publike, and private satisfacion as divinity,* **charity,** *and justice call* **for** *at your* **handes** *for all your former* **wronges.** If you will be soe spontaneously **just as to** doe me right yourself upon this my private demande of justice from you, I shall hereupon complaine noe further. *If not, I can, I shall then with greater cause and safety openly sue for justice against you to those who are able to doe me right, and to give me that recompence as your self denye me.* And thus desiring God of his infinite mercy to pardon, to purge out all **the venome, malice,** and violence of your heart against my self and others, to put bowells of mercy, pitty, meeknes, and affection towardes all good men into you, and to give you grace unfainedly to repent of **all your** *violent, unjust, extravagant, oppressive, vexatious, despitefull courses and proceedings which crye aloud for vengeance against you,* **and** *will certainly end in misery, ruyne, if not in hell it self, if* you runne on madding in them, without restraint or feare, I humbly take my leave, and rest

Your Grace's oppressed one, seeking, not grace, but justice from you,
WILLIAM PRYNNE.

From the Tower of London,
June xi. 1634.

Tit. 1, 8, &c.

Audiant hoc Prelati qui sibi commissis semper nolunt esse formidini utilitati raro. Discite subditorum matres nos esse debere non dominos. Studete magis amari, quam metui. Et si interdum severitate opus est, paterna sit non tyrannica. Matres fovendo, patres nos corripiendo exhibeatis. Mansuecite, ponite feritatem. Suspendite verbera, pro ducite ubera, pectora lacte pinguescant, non typho turgeant. Quid jugum vestrum super eis aggravatis, quorum potius contra

James 2, 13. Matth. 7, 2.

He shall have judgment without mercye that hath shewed noe mercye. With what judgment ye judge **ye shall be** judged, and with **what measure ye** mete it shall be measured to you againe.

portare debetis. **Cur** morsus a serpente parvulus fugit conscientiam sacerdotis, ad quem eum magis oportuerat tanquam ad sinum recurrere matris. Si spirituales estis instruito tales spiritu lenitatis considerans unusquisque seipsum ne et ipso tenetur. Bern. super Cant. Secu. 23.

[Indorsed in Laud's hand.]

Junii 11, 1634.

A **copye of** a letter sent **unto** me June 11, 1634, **from Mr.** Prynn; conteyning, with much libelling bitternes, a confutacion **of** what I sayd in Star Chamber at the tyme **of** his **censure, and threatning** to call for justice against me, &c.

2 (3, 6).

Junii 16, 1634. *Mondaye.*

I sent the originall of Mr. Prynne's leter to Mr. Atturnye Generall by the King's command.

Junii 17.

Mr. Atturnye sent for Mr. Prinn to his chamber, shewed hime the leter, asked hime wheather **it wear his** hand. Mr. Prinn sayd he could not tell unless he might reed it. The leter beinge given into his hand, **he** tear the leter into small peeces, and threwe it out at windowe, and sayd **that** should never rise in judgment against hime; fearing (it seemes) **an ore** tenus for this.

Junii 18, 1634.

Mr. Atturney brought hime into the **Star** Chamber, whear all thiss appeard, with shame enough **to** Mr. Prinne.

V.

EXTRACTS FROM THE PRIVY COUNCIL REGISTER.

At Whytehall the 7th of March, 1633.[a]

Present.

Lord Archbishop of Canterburie.

Lo: Keeper.	Erle of Exceter.
Lo: Treasurer.	Erle of Kellie.
Lo: Privie Seale.	Lo: Cottington.
Lo: High Chamberlain.[b]	Mr. Comptroller.[d]
Erle Marshal.[c]	Mr. Secretary Windebanck.

Warrant concerning the bringing in of Prine's Booke.

Whereas of late an infamous libell and booke called Histriomastix, full of scandall to his Majestie, his royall consort the Queene, the officers of his house, the magistrates and whole state, fraught with uncharitable and unchristian censures of all sortes of people and actions indifferently, besides manie positions dangerous to his Majestie's person, and intolerable, hath bene printed, published, and dispersed into diverse partes of this realme, for composing, printing, and publishing of which infamous and scurrillous booke and libell one Pryne the author and Michael Sparkes the printer are sentenced by the Courte of Star Chamber to undergoe, besides fyne and imprisonment, corporal and shamefull punishment, and the bookes are ordered to be burnt. Forasmuch as upon search and examination of the remembrances and accounts of the said Sparkes it appeareth how manie of the said bookes were dispersed

---

[a] *i. e.* 1633-4.
[b] The Earl of Lindsey.
[c] The Earl of Arundel.
[d] Sir Henry Vane.

PROCEEDINGS AGAINST WILLIAM PRYNNE.   59

into everie one of their hands whose names are underwritten, these are to require you to repaire to the said persons at the severall places of their dwellings, and by shewing these unto them to require everie of them to make diligent enquirie and certificate of all those to whom they have solde or dispersed any of the said bookes, and in his Majesties name commande them to deliver so manie of them as remaine in their hands unto the wardens of the Companie of Stationers, London, before the last day of this moneth, and before that time to make certificate to the said wardens of the names of all those to whom they have dispersed any of the said bookes; letting them knowe that so manie of them as shal not retourne or make certificate how those bookes have been dispersed by them upon sale or otherwise, with the names of all those to whom they have vented them, a strict accompt shalbe required of them, wherein they must expect to be charged with concealing of so manie as they shal not discover to have bene vented abroad to others, whose names they shal declare and certifie as aforesaid.

Signed as the Session.
Mr. Buckner.
Mr. Bray, my Lord's Grace of Canterbury's Chaplaine.
Mr. Prynne.
Mr. Apsly, the **Warden of the** Companie of Stationers.

Mr. Allot.	Mr. Allcorne.
Mr. Milbonne.	**Mr.** Stephens and Paul's Churchyard.
Mr. Boller.	Mr. Maydothe.
Mr. Ebb.	Mr. Ladam.
Mr. **Man.**	Mr. Doleman.
Mr. **Bostock.**	Mr. Seele.
Mr. Bobinson.	**Mr. Ritterden.**
Mr. Radway.	**Mr. Collins.**
Mr. Brewster. Pope's Head	**Mr. Overton.**
Mr. Butter. Alley.	**Mr. Allen.**
Mr. Tawne. St. Dunstane's.	**Mr. Marryot.**

Ivye Lane, by the Exchange.	Mr. Grismond.		Mr. Moore.
	Mr. Bellamy.		Mr. Butter.
Cheapside.	Mr. Barret.		Mr. Famton.
Olde Bayley.	Mr. **Edwards**.		Mr. Sheeres.
Temple Gate.	Mr. **Dawson**.		Mr. Sweyne.
by London Bridge.	Mr. **Clifton**.	Duck Lane.	Mr. **Mynne**.
Seacole Lane.	Mr. **Clever**.	Aldersgate.	Mr. Fisher.
Graye's Inn.	Mr. **Willson**.		
Cornhill.	Mr. **Clarke**.		
St. Lawrence **Lane**.	Mr. **Birde**.		
	Mr. Roqueny.		

Another warrant of the same tenor **to Oxford to the persons** whose names are hereunder specified:

	Mr. Westable.	Mr. Turner.
	Mr. Huggins.	Mr. Curtiey.
	Mr. **Aylyam**.	Mr. Bowman.
	Mr. Forrest.	Mr. Cole.
Bristol.	Mr. Thomas.	

Another to Salisbury, **Exceter,** and Dorchester, to Mr. Hammond, Mr. Dight, Mr. **Burrell**.

Another to Mr. Camson of Norwich.

Another to Mr. Whaley of Northampton, Mr. Woller of Manchester, **Mr.** Clarke and Mr. Jennings of Ludlowe, and to Mr. Steele of Nantwich.

At Whytehall the 15th of March, 1636.[a]

Present.

Lo: Archb. of Cant.
Lo: Keeper.
Lo: Trear.
Lo: Privie Seale.
Lo: High Chamberlaine.
Ea: Marshall.
Lo: Chamberlaine.
Ea: of Northumberland.
Ea: of Dorsett.

Ea: of Salisbury.
Ea: of Holland.
Lo: Cottington.
Lo: Newburgh.
Mr. Trear.[b]
Mr. Controller.[c]
Mr. V. Chamberlaine.
Mr. Sec. Coke.
Mr. Sec. Windebanke.

Whereas informacion was this day given to the board by Mr. Attourney Generall, that he had preferred a bill of complainte in the Starr Chamber against Henry Burton, clerke, and others; and that the said Mr. Burton doth refuse to make answere to the said complainte unlesse he may have liberty to goe abroad to prepare and advise with his councell, though his councell had leave to have accesse and to conferre with him in the prison; yet to take away all allegacions or pretences for excuse herein their Lordshipps have thought fitt and ordered that the said Mr. Burton shall have liberty to goe abroad with his keeper, to speake and conferre with his councell when he desireth the same; and that his said keeper is to have speciall care that the said Mr. Burton doe not make use of this liberty to conferre with other persons, and that he bee permitted to goe to noe other place but to his said councell, and that the said Mr. Burton shall ymmediatly appeare to the said bill and make aunswere within tenn dayes after, and thereupon the board will give such further order as shall bee fitt.

Mr. Burton, Prin, and Baskett;[d] liberty to aunswere in Starr Chamber.

The like order for William Prin and another for Baskett.[d]

[a] i. e. 1636-7.
[b] Treasurer of the Household, Sir Thomas Edmondes.
[c] Sir Henry Vane.   [d] Bastwick.

25th June, **1637.**

It was **this day** ordered (his Majestie being present **in Councell**) that **Mr. Atturnie** Generall shall **move in** the Starr Chamber **on** Thursday next **for** the **present execucion** of the sentence against Burton, Barstwick, and Prinne, **and that** it may be declared by the Court **that all the** three delinquents sentenced in that cause shall be kept in the severall places where **they** are to be ymprisoned without being admitted to have any use **of penn,** inke, or paper, or of any other bookes but the Bible and **the Booke** of Common Prayer, and such **other bookes** of devocion as the severall keepers **of the said castles** will be answerable for **that they be** consonant to the **doctrine** of the Church of England.

A Warrant with generall direccions.

Wm. Prynne imprisonned in Carnarvan Castle.

Whereas the Warden **of the Fleete** is by order **of the** Starr Chamber **of** the 15th of **this** present July required **to** receave from the Lieutenant of **the** Tower the body of William Prynn, **Gent. and to** cause him **to bee** carryed downe to the goale of the **Castle** of Carnarvan, and there **to** be delivered, to remaine prisoner in **that** goale, in such sorte **as by the** decree of the **said** Court of Starr Chamber is directed: **These** shall bee therefore **in his Majesty's name** straightly **to charge and** commaund you **and every of you whom** it may concerne to **be** ayding and assisting unto the said **warden** of the Fleete, his deputy, or such person **or persons as he shall** imploy for **this service,** as well in the safe conveying of the said Prynn from place **to** place untill he **come to** the said **goale,** as also in appointing sufficient guards at **nightes and** other times needfull, and **in** affording **you** best advise, **helpe,** and furtherance upon all occasions wherein the same shall **bee** required for the better execucion of this service, whereof you may not faile, as you will aunswere the contrary at your uttermost perills.

Dated the 20th of July, 1637, and signed,

Lo: Keeper.   Ea: of Morton.
Lo: High Chamberlaine.   Lo: Newburgh.
Ea: Marshall.   Mr. V. Chamberlaine.

The like Warrant for the carrying **downe** of John Bastwick, Doctor in Phisick, to the Castle of **Launceston**, in Cornwall, there to bee imprisoned, **as abovesaid. Dated and signed** *ut ante* cum Mr. Comptroller. Dr. Bastwick, prisoner in Cornewall.

The like Warrant for the carrying downe of Henry Burton **to** the Castle of Lancaster, there to bee imprisoned, &c. as above said. Dated and signed *ut ante*, **except** Mr. Controller. Mr. Burton, prisoner in Lancaster Castle.

30th of July, 1637

Whereas William Prinn **is by** the late **sentence of** the High Courte of Starre Chamber **to be comitted to the goale** in the Castle of **Carnarvon and** there to be **kept closse prisoner,** theire Lordshipps conceivinge **that the said** Prinn **cannot be in a** common goale kept so closse **a prisoner as by** the said sentence **is** intended: Upon consideracion **thereof doe** hereby will and require **John Griffith, Esquire, Constable of** the said Castle of Carnarvon, **and** his deputy, or either of them, to suffer the sheriff of the county of Carnarvon, or the keeper of the said goale under him the said **sheriffe for the** tyme being, still **to use such roome** or chamber **without the said goale and within the said castle as shall** be most **fitt and convenient for the said sheriffe** for the tyme being **or his** goaler to **keepe** the said Prinn a closse prisoner there, and that none of the other prisoners or any other person or persons **be permitted** to come into the said **castle** to conferr or any way **to converse** with **the** said William Prinn, such only excepted as **are** to take care of his safetie, or to attend the said Prinn to give him dayly sustenance **and releefe.** And the said Prinn is not to be permitted [to] have

Touching Prynn, Bastwick, and Burton.

the use of any penn, inke, or paper, **or of any booke or bookes save the Byble, the Booke of Common Prayer, and such other canonicall books as he shall desire** for his comfort or devocion, and **which are** consonant **to the** religion professed in the Church of England. In regard **of which** closse imprisonment his Majestie will give allowance for **his dyett.** For all which this order shall be a sufficient warrant to **the said John Griffith, and to his** deputy, **and** the goaler aforesaid.

Twoe lyke orders, the **one touching Mr.** Burton, **prisoner in** the Castle **of** Lancaster, the other **for Dr.** Bastwick, **prisoner in** the Castle **of** Lanceston, in the county of Cornwall.

At the Court att **Oatelands** the 27th of **August, 1637.**

Present.

The King's **Most** Excellent Majesty.

Lo: Arch. of Cant.	Ea. of Dorsett.
Lo: Keep.	Ea. of Holland.
Lo: Trear	Lo. V. Wimbledon.
Lo: Duke of Lenox.	Mr. Comptroler.
Lo: Marq. Hamilton.	Mr. **Sec.** Coke.
Ea. Marshall.	Mr. **Sec.** Windebank.

Ordered the 27th; Touching Bastwick, Burton, and Prinn.

Whereas by sentence and decree of the Court of Starr Chamber, John Bastwick, Henry **Burton,** and William Pryne, were committed lately to remayne **close prisoners;** the said **John** Bastwick in the **Castle** of Lanceston, **Henry Burton** in the Castle of Lancaster, **and** William Prine in the **Goal or Castle of** Carnarvon. His Majestie haveing **bin** since informed **how** inconvenient the said places are for the custodie and guard of those prisoners, did this day order, **with the** advise of the **Board, that** the said Bastwicke should be **removed to** the Castle or Fort of the Isles of Sillies, Burton to the **Castle of the Island of Guernescy, and** Prinne to one of the two **Castles** of the Isle of **Jarsey (which by the** governor of the same shalbe thought fittest), to be there safely kept **closse prisoners in ther chambers;** and that to prevent the daunger **of spreading their schismaticall** and seditious opinions (which was the cause **wherefore** the Court of Starr Chamber did imprison them in those **remote places**) none **be admitted to have conference with** them or to have accesse unto them, but only such **as being** faithfull and discreet **persons shalbe** appoynted by **the governor or captuines** of those **castles or their deputies for attendance uppon them, to give** them theire daylie sustenance and necessaryes; **nor they the said prisoners** are not to be allowed **the use of any penn, paper, or incke, nor of** any bookes but only **of the Bible, the Book of** Common **Prayer,** and suche bookes which **they shall desire, for** the practise **and exercise of** private devotion **only, the** same to be **alsoe such as the** said governors, captaines, **or their** deputyes, know **to be consonant to the doctrine and discipline established in the Church of England,** and for which they will **be** answerable **to his Majestie that the same are such.** And that **no letters nor writings be** permitted to be **brought unto the said prisoners, nor from them to be** sent to any person or place **whatsoever. And if there shalbe any such brought, that the same** be opened **by the said governors, captaines, or their** deputyes, and, if they **containe any thing materiall or considerable,** that the same be sent to **one of His Majestie's Principall Secretaryes.** And moreover that the wives **of the said Bastwick and Burton, who (as His Majestie hath been informed) have made some attempts** to procure accesse unto ther said husbands, **and to conveigh** lettres **unto them,** and is conceaved **wilbe evill** instruments to disperse and scatter **abroad these** dangerous opinions **and** designs, which ther said husbands shall **desire** to spread, contrary to the true intent **of** the sentence and decree of the said Court, therfore they shall not **be** permitted to **land nor** abide in any of the said islands. **And if** contrary hereunto it **should** happen through the inadvertency of officers or otherwise that they or either of them should land in any of the said islands, that the same being discovered **and** made knowne to the respective governors or captaines **of** the same, or unto the deputies of the said governors and captaines respectively, they or either of them soe offending should be forthwith committed to prison, there to be detayned untill further order from the board. And it is further ordered that those persons who shalbe employed for removeing the said persons as aforesaid, either by sea or land, doe carry or conveigh them with all privacy and secrecy to prevent all concourse of people in their passage; and that they suffer noe person whatsoever but themselves only, who have the care and charge of conveying them, to speak with them in their passage.

At the Court at Oatlands the 10th day of September, 1637.

Present.

The King's Most Excellent Majesty.

Lo: Arch Bpp. of Cant.	Ea: of Dorsett.
Lo: Treasurer.	Ea: of Holland.
Lo: Marques Hamilton.	Lo: Cottington.
Ea: Marshall.	Mr. Sec. Coke.

Mr. Sec. Windebank.

Mr Atturney to take examinacions about Prynn and Burton.

Whereas Mr. Sollicitor Generall hath by his Majestie's commands taken examinacions concerning the greate concourse of people which were permitted to resort unto and converse with William Prynne and Henry Burton in the places where they staid or lodged in their passage to the places of imprisonment (to which by sentence in Star Chamber they were committed): Forasmuch as Mr. Sollicitor is now imployed in other his Majestie's service soe as hee cannot goe through with the examinacion of that matter, it was therefore this day ordered (his Majestie present in Councell) that Mr. Atturney Generall shal bee hereby prayed and required forthwith to proceed in examinacion as well of the Warden of the Fleet and his deputy as of such persons as were by either of them imployed in the carrying and conveying the said Prynn and Burton to the places of their imprisonment, or of any others, whereby to discover what persons did accompany, converse with, or entertaine

either of them in their said passage, what money **was given to**
them, or either of them, or other remarkable expressions of
courtesie or encouragement were shewed to either of them, **by**
whome, **at what places, and how** often in their way, and any thing
els that may make knowne the persons and dispositions of those
that resorted to the said Prynne and Burton in their way to their
said imprisonment. Whereof Mr. Atturney is make certificate to
the boord in writing with convenient speed, **to th'end** that such
further course may bee taken therein as shal bee fitt.

A Letter directed to the High Sherrife of the county of
Lancaster.

Whereas his Majestie with the advice of this boord hath given order
that Henry Burton (who by sentence and decree of the Court of
Star Chamber was lately committed to remaine close prisoner in the
Castle **of Lancaster) shal bee** removed to the Castle of the Isle of
Guernesey, there to bee kept prisoner according to an order of this
boord untto his Majestie's Governour of the said Isle; wee are, by
his Majestie's especiall command to require and charge you forthwith **to take effectuall order that the said Henry Burton bee with**
all diligence and safety embarqued **in some convenient port or**
place in that county nearest to **the castle where now hee is prisoner,**
and thence with the first opportunity **of wind** transported, at his
Majestie's charge, by such faithfull **and trusty** officers **as** you will
answere for, his Majestie's Isle of Guernesey, **and** there safely deli-
vered into the charge and custody of the Governor **or** Lieutenant
Governor **of the** said Isle, **to bee** kept close prisoner **in** the castle
there, **according to** the said order. And to this purpose wee have
herein sent **you a warrant to the** keeper of the Castle **of Lancaster**
to deliver the said **Burton to you, or such as you shall appoint to**
receave him, into **custody;** and doe **hereby authorise and** require
you to presse and take up such shipp or **barke as** you shall find fitt
for the said Henry Burton's transportacion, paying such price for

the same as shall be reasonable, **the charge of** whose **remove** and transportacion shal bee allowed unto you upon your accompt. **You are to see** that the vessell you take up or presse for this **purpose bee** ready fitted to put to sea before you take the said Burton out of the prison where **now** he remains, and **to** take effectuall care and **order** that the persons whom **you imploy** for removing the said **Burton, as aforesaid** (either **by sea or land), doe carry** and conveigh him with all privacy and secrecy, and without making any unnecessary stop **or** stay, **to prevent all** concourse **of** people in his passage, and **that** they permitt **noe person** whatsoever (but **themselves who have** the care and charge of removing him) **to speak with** him in **his** passage; and wee doe hereby will and **command all mayors, vice** admirals, justices of peace, customers, comptrollers, **searchers,** marshalls of the admiralty, constables, and **other** his Majestie's officers and subjects, to bee ayding and assisting unto you **in the due execucion of this our** warrant. And this shall **be a** sufficient warrant both to you and them on this behalfe. And soe wee bid, &c. Dated **the 17th of September, 1637.** Signed by,

Lo: Arch Bpp. of Cant.   Ea: of Northumberland.
Lo: Keeper.   Ea: of Dorsett.
Lo: Treasurer.   Lo: Cottington.
Lo: Privie Seale.   Mr. Comptroller.
Lo: Marquis Hamilton.   Mr. Sec. Coke.
Ea: Marshall.   Mr. Sec. Windebank.

A **letter of** the like **tenor** was directed **to** the High Sherriffe of the **County of** Carnarvon **for** the removing of William Prinne from the **Goale or** Castle **of** Carnarvon, to bee transported to one of the **two Castles** of the **Isle of** Jersey, **which** by the governour of the **same shalbee** thought fittest, **to be there** kept close prisoner. Dated **and signed** *ut ante*.

A like letter was sent to the High **Sherrife of** the County of **Cornewell** for the removing of John **Bastwick from** the Goal or **Castle of** Launceston, **in** the county aforesaid, to His Majestie's

Castle or Fort in the Isle of Silley, there to bee kept close prisoner. Dated and signed as the two former.

A **Warrant to the Keeper or** Under-Keeper of the Castle of Lancaster.

It is his Majestie's pleasure that you forthwith deliver the person of Henry Burton (formerly by sentence of the Court of Star Chamber ordered to be kept prisoner in the Castle **of Lancaster**) unto the High Sherrife of the county of Lancaster, or to such person as hee shall appoint to receave and take the said Burton into custody, for which this shal bee your warrant. Dated the 17th of September, and signed *ut ante*.

The like Warrant to the Constable of the Goal **or Castle** of **Carnarvon**, or his lieutenant or deputy, to **deliver William Prynne** to the High Sherrife of the county of Carnarvon.

Another like Warrant, to the Keeper or Under-keeper of the Goale or **Castle of Launceston, to deliver John** Bastwick to the High **Sherrife of the county of Cornewall.**

VI.

NEWS-LETTERS FROM C. ROSSINGHAM.

[State Papers, Domestic, ccclxi. 92.]

15 June, 1637.

The last Wensdaie the warrant was signed to carry **my Lord Moone to the** Fleete upon **the** sentence of the Star Chamber, but he did onely paie **the** 10^{li} fee to the warden, and is to enter into bonds to paie the King his fine of 500^{li}, so to be releast of course. It was observed, the same daye the sentence was given, that there was **not one ill** word spoaken **in** disgrace of Sir James Bagg, as had **bine formerly** spoaken at **severall motions,** as alsoe when the sentence past upon Sir James Bagg in **that cause** where Sir Anthony **Pell was** plaintive; **now, the reason is said** to bee that his Majestie has given order **that noe bitter** language should be spoaken in **disgrace** of these persons **in question,** but **that their Lordships should** discharge their **consciences in their** sentences **with all freedome whatsoever.** Fridaie **last,** some Aldermen of **London,** with their **Recorder and some of the** Common Council, **were all** before **the Lords of** the Councell **about** their composition **for** London **Derry, in** Ireland, and **other differences his** Majestie hath with the **citty.** Their Lordships told them the Kinge **was** gratiously pleasd not **to take** the extreamity **of lawe** against them, but **to** take a composition, which hee **would have** concluded on before his progress. They humbly told **their Lordships how the** business **stood betweene his** Majestie and them, **that they had** offered in the **Common Councell one** hundred twelve **thousand five hundred pounds to** cleare **all** differences, to **paie it by ten** thousand pounds yearely, but **his Majestie** prest **to have it by twenty thousand** pounds yearely

till it were paid, and to have their fishing, which yielded **the citty**
900ᵗⁱ yearely rent: As for the fishing, they told their **Lordships if**
the Kinge would have it then the citty did humbly desire **to be**
excused for giving **the** 112,500ᵗⁱ, which the Companies would not
yield **unto.** This not pleasing his Majestie, they had offered, naye,
they **had humbly besought** his Majestie, **to take** the plantacion of
London Derry **with all royalties** whatsoever, with all the arreres of
rent, which rents amounts unto twenty thousand pounds, or there-
abouts; besides, they will give his Majestie over and above all this,
ten thousand pounds more, to be forthwith paid. The Kinge hath
bine formerly acquainted with this offer, but for some reasons it
was not presently imbracst, but it is hopt and believd his Majestie
will nowe accept of it, it being suppos'd his Majestie hath **receavd**
good incouragement from Ireland, that within fewe yeares **the**
London Derry plantation maye be improvd to **be a reasonable por-**
tion for some of his Majestie's younger children. **All that was**
done that daye was, their Lordships dismist the cittizens, promising
to acquaint his Majestie with their offer, and within a few daies
after they should have his Majestie's aunsweare. The same daye
my Lord's Grace proposd to some of the Aldermen and Common
Councell of London the herring fishing upon **the coast; that the**
citty would sett upp the trade of fishing, that the Dutch might **not**
carry away the honour and profitt of soe rich a commodity, **which**
did more properly belonge to the people of **England.** His Grace
said he would commend that worke to the citty, even with the
same zeale as he had recommended **the repaireing** of the Cathedral
Church of St. Paul, and he would impute it as one of his greatest
happinesses **if he** could persuade the citty to undertake that fishing
heartily. **One of** the Aldermen having a full licence of his Grace
to speake freely, told **their** Lordships the citty **would never under-**
take it, being much better imployd in the **more marchantable** and
richer commodities of the kingdome, as **namely,** cloath, tyn and
lead, and such like, which, **if so be the** Dutch could so well trade
in as we can, they would **noe more fish** for herrings than we doe;

besides the Dutch did fish for **necessity of food**, and, God be
thanked, we **had noe** such necessity, **neither** will the **people** of
England **cate fish**, although they are commanded thereunto at
tymes **appointed.** Alderman **Garwaye** alleadgd soe **many good
reasons against his** Grace's propositions as it is believd the citty **will
be noe more prest to** undertake that work; this Alderman assure-
ing **their Lordships** they bought **herrings of the** Dutch, to trade
with them in the Straights, **at much easier rates then they** could
take them by fishing. The **last weeke his Majestie sent a com-**
mand to those of the parish **of St. Gregories by Paulls,** that **because**
Paulls Church could not be repaired a long that **side where St.**
Gregories Church standeth, as alsoe that it was not fitting the
Cathedral Church of St. Paull should be coopt upp by other buildings whatsoever, and for some other reasons, therefore his Majestie's
commaund was, that church should be pulld downe before Michael-
mas next. Sondaie last the parishieners petitiond his Majestie that
their church might not **be** pulld downe; first, because they know
not where to sett it **upp** againe; alsoe, they had lately bestowed
1700li to repaire and beautifie **it; alsoe, that** church of St. Gregorie
was more ancient then that of St. Paull by 80 yeares at least, it
having bine a church 617 yeares; notwithstanding their **petition,**
it must goe down by the tyme appointed. This church does not
belonge to this parish, but to the petty cannons of **Paulls,** whoe
rent it out to them, tithes and all, for 40 yearely rent, and a fine
of 200 at the end of **every three yeares;** the very truth is, as this
church stands a greate **parte of Paulls cannot be** repair; besides,
this church putts Paulls **Church out of all** uniformity, which being
once removd, it is resolvd that cathedrall shall **be** reducst to a
uniformity with the **est end,** with butteresses, and pinnacles. **Sir
John Strangwayes or** Strangwish, of Dorsettshire, Sir Lewis
Dives, and Sir Edw. Stradling, these three are **served** with sub-
pœnas out of the Star Chamber to aunsweare **to an** information
which is to be exhibited there against them at the King's suite, but
in Mr. Attorneye's name, for transporting of gould out of the

kingdome; the bill is not yet come in. I do **heare, these three**
knights went over sea some yeares since with **my Lord Digby, and**
that they carryed alonge with them 40^{li} a peece in gould **for their**
private expences, **which** I heare **is** more then the statute **does**
allowe, but **of this more** hereafter when the bill comes into Court.
Sondaye last the Bishopp **of** Lincolne petitiond his Majestie in the
presence at Greenewich for one fortnight's longer tyme to instruct
his councell; the King tooke the petition, putt off his hatt, gave it to
my Lord Keeper, but noe **longer tyme will** be allowed, the Kinge
haveing given a commaund **to all his** lords to attend upon Fridaye
next the heareing of that cause, which will take upp all this terme,
and some **daies** after the terme; besides, I heare by some **of** the
Bishopp's **owne** counsell **that have perusd** the bookes that **it** will
goe **very hard** with him. **There is** a contention fallen **out betweene**
the two citties **of** London and Norwich thus: **the Lord Maior of**
London hath elected an Alderman of Norwich, Atkins, that **is to**
be Maior of Norwich, this next yeare to be Sheriffe **of** London, and
hee will hold, though it **be** much to his charge; the city of Norwich will not lett him goe, they therefore **have** sent upp four **of**
their aldermen to petition the Kinge against the city of London,
whoe **will alsoe** maintaine their priviledges, **to choose where they**
please any that are freemen of London; the **petition was read on**
Sondaie last, and referred **to be ended at the Councell boord.** This
Atkins laye by the heeles almost halfe a yeare because hee refusd
to weare his owne armes at **a generall muster** in Norwich before
my **Lord** Maltravers, since hee was an alderman of that citty; this
is said to be one reason why hee **would** remove. Another reason
is, **because** very many of the cittizens of Norwich are sommond into
the Chauncellour's **court** there for not conformeing to some **late**
orders made by the **Bishopp of** that diocesse in his late visitation;
as alsoe, because there **is** very litle preaching **in Norwich, four** or
five lectures upon the weeke daies being putt downe, and noe sermons in the afternoones upon Sondaies, and **but one in the** morne-
ing through the citty; but certainely that **is** not soe, because there

bee forty or fifty churches within that citty. Saterdaye last, my Lord of Leicester's secretarie, Mounsier Batier, came to the court; hee brought over, under the French King's hand and seale, a confirmation of all those Articles sent over by his Majestie, so that nowe the confederacy betweene the twoe Kings of England and France is really concluded; but what these Articles are, that we are not certaine of; but these reports there are abroade, namely, that the two Kings are joynd in a league offensive and defensive against the house of Austria, but with some restrictions on our parte in the league offensive against the Spaniards. Others saye, by this confederacy the Kinge is to send into Germany ten thousand men to paie them; alsoe to send eight thousand more to the French, but the French Kinge to paie them. This report is given out by some of the Prince Elector's followers, who are overjoyd that the Prince Elector and his brother goe to Holland this next weeke, for soe it was resolvd on uppon Sonday night last, his Majestie sitting in Councell with the Junto uppon forraine affaires, for upon Mondaye the Prince Elector and his brother sent into the citty, where they owed any mony, to have the bills brought in that they might be dischargd before their going over sea. Another report is, the French Kinge hath bound himselfe to conclude noe peace with the house of Austria, but first to include the Prince Elector, his lands and dignities, and not without the consent of the Kinge of England, whoe is, upon the French King's confirmation of these Articles, to declare himself according to an agreement. It is said that some messinger shall be forthwith sent to the Emperour to demaund the Palatinates and the Electorate, and to give his Imperiall Majestie notice of this confederacy. Mondaie last the Commissioners about compositions for the lands in Essex forrest sate at my Lord Treasurer's; divers freeholders compounded. Doctor Wright, the phisitian, gave a 100 markes to free 200^{li} yearely rents from the forrest lawes, though he had an Act of Parliament to exempt those lands many yeares since, but hath gotten free warren into the bargaine, which hee had not before; some others there were that compounded, and there is noe question but all the gentry will come in; but what the peasants will doe that is not yet knowne; when they meete together they talke at large, but being devided they soone become crest fallen to doe what shall be required of them. I doe not yet heare what is done to those gentlemen of Essex which subscribd that letter which was, that by reason of the late heavy charges they had not wherwithall to compound if they had a desire thereunto. Wensdaie this week Dr. Bastwicke, Mr. Burton, and Mr. Prin were brought to the Star Chamber barr; the information against them taken *pro confesso*. They all spake somewhat for themselves, but to noe purpose. Dr. Bastwicke cast an aunsweare into the Court four yards longe and a yard broade, close written. Prin offered his aunsweare, subscribed by councell, but it came too late; and all Mr. Burton's aunsweare but five lines was expungd, which five lines hee renounest. The court examined whether Prin had any eares left; they found they were cropt, soe they went to sentence; my Lord Cottington began and find them 5 or 6,000^{li} a peece; to loose their eares in the pillory at Westminster; Prin to have the rest of his eares cutt of, and to perpetuall imprisonment in the Castle of Carnarvon, in Wales. Dr. Bastwick to be imprisond in the Castle of Lestwithyn, in Cornewall; and Burton in the Castle of Lancaster; these two last to be degraded, and all of them to communicate with none but by order of that court. Twenty-two lords gave sentence, the Kinge sending the court lords from Theobalds that morneing to give sentence. Lord of London past noe sentence, but would do good for evill, and prayd that God would give them *mentem saniarem*;[a] soe did his Grace, but hee spake two howers out of a note booke prepard for that purpose against Burton's aunsweare, which was invectives against innovations in the Church, which his Grace devided into fourteen heads; justificing removeing of table alterwise by Queen Elizabeth's injunctions; boweing at the name

[a] *Sic.*

of Jesus out of the Cannon, even in sermon time; doeing reverence at the communion table, as a thing most fitting, but noe body had bine forcst to it, nor to remove the table but by perswasion; his Grace refuted the Bishopp's booke lately publisht, the Bishopp of Lincolne being present to heare it, where his Grace said the Bishopp was mistaken, and that as learned as himselfe were of that oppinion. His Grace past no sentence, but gave the lords thankes that did passe the sentence upon those delinquents. My Lord Chiefe Justice Finch sentencst Prin to be branded in the forehead with an S. and a L. for a seditious libellour, and this was the sentence of the whole Court. Expungd out of Mr. Burton's aunsweare by both the Chiefe Justices to whom it was referred, all.[a]

[State Papers, Domestic, ccclxii. 31.]

22 JUNE, 1637.

There are about fifty several Commissions under the Privy Seale directed to the Costos Rotulorum of every county throughout England and Wales, requireing them to make inquiry what misdemeanors have bine committed by inkeepers, alehousekeepers, and victuallers of all sorts contrarye to such recognizances as they have entred into for the keeping of good orders. And where they find any forfeitures they have power by this Commission to compound with the said delinquents, to take 20^s for the forfeiture of every recognizance. If any victualler shall refuse to compound at this rate, the Costos Rotulorum must retourne their forfeited recognizances into the Exchequer. This Commission looks back many yeares; and as many recognizances as any one man hath entered into, soe many severall 20^s hee must paye. There are two other Commissions ordered to be drawne upp, to passe the Privy Seale;

[a] The MS. breaks off here.

one is, to make inquiry into the breach of the statute, that noe
scrivener shoull take above 5ˢ brokadge in the £. Alsoe I heare
there is some clauses to be inserted into this Commission, that will
fall upon the usurour, to gett some mony from him alsoe. This
Commission will bee onely to drawe mony from the scriveners, and
afterwards they committ the same sinnes again more boldly then
before. There is a third Commission to compound with all such as
have erected cottages contrary to the statute, which is, to laye four
acres of land to every cottage. This Commission lookes back to
the thirtieth of Queen Elizabeth. The depopulation Commission
is for the distroying of familes, and this of cottages is for over
peopling of townes. The Kinge sent a commaund to the Barons
of the Exchequer to heare once againe the cause depending in that
court betweene Mr. William Murrey, of the Bedchamber, and Sir
John Hippisly. It was heard the last terme and ordered then
that Sir John Hippisly should account for noe more of these repri-
sall goods then came to his hand, and that hee should not account
by the bills of ladeing, as Mr. Murrey would have had it. Also,
that the auditors were to examine Sir John Hippislye's account;
the last weeke it was heard againe, as his Majestie commaunded,
and as it was ordered at the first heareing soe it was againe at the
second heareing, nothing altered. Fridaye last the Aldermen and
Common Councell of the city of London appeared at the board by
sommons about the composition, where their Lordships signified
his Majesty's pleasure, that it should bee at the choise of the citty
of London which of their two propositions they should stand to, to
compound all differences. The Comon Councell told their Lordships they did most willingly surrender into his Majesty's hands
their whole plantacion of London Derry, with all the royalties and
arreeres of rents and the 10,000ˡⁱ over and above, which his Majestie hath accepted of, soe the Kinge hath at present noe further
difference with the city of London. What Mr. St. John, the
lawyer of Lincolnes Inn, hath lately done I cannot yet heare, but
somewhat there is against him, by reason of the consequencies, for
upon Sondaye last a warrant was signd by the Lords of the Coun-

cell, verie many hands to this warrant, which was **given to Sir
William Beacher, clarke** of the Councell, to goe forthwith to **London** to search for papers in Mr. St. John's study in Lincolnes Inn;
because there were soe many papers therefore they were all seasd
uppon and brought thence by a porter, with a cabbinet which
could not well be opened at that tyme. I heare all Mr. St. John's
notes about the argument of the shipp writt (for hee was one of the
assignd counsell for my Lord Saye, that hath putt in his information into the King's Bench against the constable that destraynd his
catle for non payement of shipp money). I heare all those notes
are amongst **his** other papers carryed awaye. Alsoe, Mr. St. **John**
is said **to have** bine a diligent searcher of records concerneing
forrest bounds and lawes, and that hee had collected, or at least
supposed to have collected, some choyse manuscripts, all which,
after that is found which is searcht for, shall be restord him, but
good tyme **will** be required before all his volumes of papers can be
perusd. I doe not heare that the argument about the shipp writt is
to bee argued this terme, soe my Lord Saye shall not bee prejudicst,
because, before the next terme, his counsell shall have his papers
restord, or may in the meane tyme recollected[a] them againe. I
wrote in my last how Sir John Strangwish and others were in the
Star Chamber for transporting of gould; the bill is nowe come in,
and one clausse in yt is, the Attorney maye bringe into **the same**
bill as many more defendants as he shall discover; besides these
three knights there are some others lately servd. The some chargd
in the bill is noe lesse then 200,000 pounds, and Mr. Kylvert
does sollicite this cause. This busines is like to fall heavy uppon
some of the defendants, but I heare Sir John Strangwish does very
much slight it. Fridaye last, the bill against the Bishopp of Lincolne was opened in the Star Chamber by Mr. Serjeant Whitfeild;
the charges were very fowle and exprest to the life; the Bishopp
was not spared one jott, but that shewed the serjeant's zeale to doe
his Majestie service. **The charges were six,** breifly these; first,

* *Sic.*

for procureing papers from the Councell Chamber, which ought to have bine conceald; secondly, for drawing wittnesses to varie from their former depositions; thirdly, for scandalizing Sir John Mounson and corrupting wittnesses; fourthly, Catlin's affedavit, a verie libell and procured by the Bishopp; fifthly, practice with wittnesses to smother the truth; sixthly, for affronting Mr. Kylvert and other wittnesses at a Commission, the Bishopp calling Kylvert, ignorant bace fellowe, and one of the Bishopp's servants challengd Mr. Kylvert into the feild: these be the charges, and to prove or rather to discreeditt one of the Bishopp's cheife wittnesses many depositions were read that daye, which did not satisfie the expectacion of the Court, insomuch as some of the Court lords were extreame wearie, and, as I heare, have desired the Kinge they maye bee spard from heareing any more of the cause. It is said this cause was sett downe for heareing before the Kinge's Councell had perusd the bookes, which was Mr. Kylvert's fault, who would sett it downe for heareing before the breviates were made, onely because this terme should not bee lost. Mr. Attorny prest it uppon the Bishopp by waye of aggravation, that subornation to perjury was death *intra leges Cornubiæ*. Sundaye last, uppon some incouragement given to the Bishopp, hee wrote a letter to his Majestie, most humbly casting himselfe at the King's mercy, beseecheing his Majestie that bill against him might bee noe further prosecuted, and it was hopt his Majestie would take this cause into his owne breast, if some of the Bishopp's enimies did not importune his Majestie that the cause should goe on, the depositions being very full to prove all the charges against him; which depositions could not be read the first daie, which daye was spent in readeing other depositions to introduce these. It was but a vaine hope the Bishopp had, for the cause does goe forward, his Majestie being ever resolvd to have it openly heard, and thus I heare yt. I heare the Bishopp is soe diffident in his owne cause that he gives himselfe for a lost man, and therefore as a dying man hee hath disposd of his personall estate, and hath bine his owne executor, to give legacies to

his freinds and rewards to his servants before the Star Chamber
judgment does fall uppon him, to take it from him. His revenues
as Bishopp he cannot alter, and for his other reall estate the King's
officers will find that out, to be responsable for the King's fine.
The Bishopp hath done all hee can to gaine tyme, for hee examined
200 or 300 wittnesses against the creditt of some of the King's
wittnesses in this cause against him; by a late order of the Court
those depositions were referred to both the Cheife Judges, the
Cheife Baron, and two other Judges, whoe have expungd whole
volumes of those depositions as scandalous and impertinent and contrary to the order of Court, which gave the Bishopp leave to
examine the creditt of those the King's witnesses; yet those judges
have not perusd all the depositions referred unto them. This cause
will take upp some daies after the terme. Tuesdaye last the
Lewetenant of the Tower preferred a peticion of Mr. Prin's to his
Majestie, wherein his Majestie was most humbly besought to take
it into his royall consideracion that he had not bine refractorie in
aunswearing to Mr. Attorney's information against him for which
hee was condemnd, as alsoe as guilty of those charges in that information; but hee alleadgd in this petition that hee had ingrost his
aunsweare in tyme, and his counsell had subscribd it, but before
hee could putt this aunsweare into Court his counsell had blotted
out their names againe, and before hee could drawe upp and
ingrosse an other aunsweare the tyme lymitted by the Court was
out, soe the bill against him was taken *pro confesso;* his Majestie
read this peticion and putt it upp in his pockett, but I doe not yet
heare what is done in it. Tuesdaye this weeke my Lord Powys
and Sir John Maynard were at fistecuffes in the bowleing ground.
Lord Chamberlaine was present; the quarrell began thus: Sir John
Maynard demaunded of Jack Craven (by that name hee is best
knowne) 20^{li} debt, which Mr. Craven would not acknowledge.
Maynard said nothing in reply, till Craven took his tyme to aske
him the cause why hee demaunded a debt of him in such a disgracefull manner, being alsoe not due. Maynard said then, it was

due, and Craven told him it was false, **soe the quarrell began.** Maynard stroake Craven with his fist; then **comes in Lord Powys** to part them; soe gott two or three blowes of **Sir John Maynard,** which putt his **Lordship not a little out** of patience; but Lord Chamberlaine **made upp** the businesse, and Sir John Maynard was **very penitent to my Lord** Powys, who forgave **him with** very much **a doe.** Saterdaie last one Googe, younge **sonne to Dr.** Googe, minister of **the Blackfriers, in** London, **was found dead in** the Thames, at Ivye bridge **in the Strand. It** appeard hee was first strangled, then **stabd in the breast and necke** nigh the throate; those stabs in the **breast did not passe** through either dublett or shirt, although both were upon him. **Hee** was mist all Fridaye, from ten a clocke till hee was found dead; a very orderly **younge** man for ought any body knewe; hee went out **to gett in some** debts, being a mercer in Pater noster Rowe. **One Captain Blundill** is clapt upp in Newgate upon suspicion, to whome hee was to **goe** for mony; but I **heare Dr. Googe** is fully of opinion that the captain **is inocent.**

June 22th, 1637.

[State Papers, Domestic, ccclxii. 76.]

29 JUNE, 1637.

There is a greate differences fallen out betweene **the Courts of King's Bench and the** Stanneries, thus: one Mr. Conocke being committed **by my** Lord Chamberleine's subwarden (his Lordshipe, Judge of the Stanneries), removes the cause by a writt **of habeas** corpus into the King's Bench **the** last terme. Lord **Chamberleine** committs Conocke againe, **and** the judges of **the** King's Bench graunts him another habeas corpus. Then **Conocke** enters his action of false imprisonment against **Mr. Corriton** the subwarden, whoe was to shewe cause the 20th of **June,** but fayleing, the judges ordered judgment should be entered Mondaye the 26th followeing. The same daye my Lord Chamberleine causd an injunction to bee servd in his owne name upon the councell at the King's Bench barr; they possesse the Court; an affidavitt is read; the judges take this in greate indignation, the rather because this injunction was in my Lord's owne name, whereas my Lord Keeper does ever send them in *Carol. Rege.* They alsoe declard if they were not righted in this they would all resign upp their pattents. They sent for Mr. Corriton to the barr and committ him prisoner to the King's Bench, alsoe they deliver Conocke out of my Lord Chamberlein's officer's hands. Tuesdaie my Lord gives his warrant to sease into his officer's hands Sir John Lentoll, that keepes the King's Bench Prison, a tipstaffe, and the martiall of the Court, whoe was arrested as hee went before my Lord Cheife Justice, which, saye oure lawyers, was the greatest affront that was ever offered to a Lord Cheife Justice. Alsoe a letter is delivered from the Kinge to all the judges sitting in court, commaunding them to repaire to his Majestic to Greenewich, which they did the same daye, my Lord Cheife Justice Finch goeing a long with them. In the Counsell Chamber the judges appeare, and relate to his Majestie all that had past, telling his Majestie the lawe; and howe much they wrongd and the court affronted. The King is not well pleased his judges should bee soe dealt withal; saith he, I will have the common lawe mayntaind, for that maintaines his authority; hee soe farr excuseth my Lord Chamberleine as to saye hee did beleive hee did err by councell; my Lord Chamberleine tells what councell advisd him to : but Mr. Justice Bartley[a] tells my Lord Chamberleine hee should doe well to beg the King's mercy, haveing done that hee cannot aunsweare. The Kinge orders that the King's Bench shall have the heareing of that cause, and that Corriton and Conocke bee both bound over to aunsweare yt there this next terme. The cause why Mr. St. John's papers were seasd uppon was, a complaint made to the Board, that it was not possible Mr. Burton

[a] Berkeley

should drawe his aunsweare to Mr. Attornyes soe lawyerlike as it was done without the helpe of some lawyer, and there **was** greate presumptions that Mr. St. John was that lawyer; upon which **pre**-sumption that warrant was graunted to examine his papers to see what might be discovered, for the aunsweare was soe untrue and soe scandalous, as that lawyer deservd a severe punishment that **had** his hand in **yt.** But before Mr. St. John parted with his papers hee bundled upp together all those loose notes concerning the argument about the shipp writt, that **my** Lord Saye's defences might not be to seeke when there was use of them, all **which he** ashewerd to Sir Willyam Beecher that they were the same; then he seald them under six seales, that they might not be knowne before hand, which the Lords did well eneugh like of, **and sent** them back agayne seald upp within two or three daies after **to Mr. St.** John with out opening of them. I doe not heare there are **any** papers found concerning Mr. Burton's aunsweare, neither is there any thing yet laid to Mr. St. John's **charge.** Munday last my Lord Sayes putt into court his demurrer to the constable's plea, which was the King's writt, by vertue of which writt he pleades hee did distrayne my Lord Saye's catle for non-payement of the shipp money. Lord Saye's demurrer is, that the King's writ is not sufficient to warrant the constable to take distresses; **upon this, an** argument must followe hereafter. My Lord Grace's speeche, which was spoaken in the Star Chamber at the sensure of Doctor Bast-wicke, Mr. Burton, and Mr. Prin, **in full** aunsweare of all those innovations of church ceremonies which Mr. Burton objects in his aunsweare where in hee taxeth his Grace, is now in print, wherein his Grace **offers** to justifie upon oath every particular of that speech to be true, that there is noe innovation, but all things done **accord**-ing to the rubricke and Queen Elizabeth's injunctions; **this booke is** bought upp so fast as they are not to be gotten. Saterdaye last my Lord Mountnorrys was at court; he kist the King's hands; he does putt into the Star Chamber his aunsweare **to my** Lord Deputie's bill against him, Sir Peirce Crosby, and others, for conspireing together to give it out that my Lord **Deputy beate** a man in Ireland with a cudgell, of which beating, they report, the man dyed soone after. The maulting business goes on, but with some restrictions, for now it shall be allowed that any man may malt his owne barly, either for his owne expence or to sell it in the markett; but none but such as shall be allowed must buy barly to malt it. I heare his Majestie told the Northfolcke men nothing should be done against the lawe, and alsoe there should be respect had to their conveniences; onely thus hee told them, they should not speake by their councell, for that his Majestie had advised already with his councell learned and was very well satisfied, and that the business should goe on, and, if they had any thing to saye for the better accommodateing of this malting for their countie of Northfolcke, they might speake, but not to speake at all against the project itselfe, for that was fixt and not to be altered. Fridaye last the Bishopp of Lincolne had noe good daye in the Star Chamber, some things being there objected, which his councell will have much a doe to wash off. There is no question but the Bishopp hath bine to busie in tampering with wittnesses; besides, it appears the Bishopp hath had too much dealing with meane bace fellowes, who have had a great commaund in his house, and these are the men that do sweare most against him. The same daye the King's councell producst a paper of instructions which the Bishopp was charged to have given to the defendants to learne by it howe to aunsweare the interrogatories. It was called the Bishopp's Catechisme, but the other title is, Termes for aunsweareing interrogatories, which is devided into fourteen heades; soe many of the heads as I can remember I shall sett downe, for the court hath forbidden any coppies to bee given out: first, in what termes to denye the whole interrogatorie; secondly, howe to aunsweare to one part and to denye the rest; thirdly, howe to denye memorye, to sweare uppon such a point; fourthly, whether in case hee maye referr to his aunsweare and how; fifthly, what to paye[a] a Com-

---

[a] The word was originally written so, but there is a line over it, which may be meant for an "s"; if so, it perhaps ought to be "what to saye to," which makes grammar of the following sentence.

missioner that shall presse him to sweare or to remember himselfe; sixthly, what to an interrogatorie if hee have **bine instructed or** taught what to aunsweare; seventhly, what to an interrogatorie, nothing appertaineing to the bill or aunsweare; eighthly, did you depose to such a thing, and to these words; ninethly, if you be asked any matter, putt it into your aunsweare already. These are all that I can learne, but there are severall aunsweares which I cannot gett. This catechisme comes in by the by, and being noe charge in the bill, the Bishopp cannot bee questiond for it now; but I heare Mr. Attorney does purpose to keepe it for another **bill.** In the meanetyme this catechisme does make the Bishopp the more fowle; but hee hath not made yet any of his defences. The Court sitts after the terme to end this cause, the two Cheife Justices haveing putt off the assizes till the 11th of July, ells the Kinge would have done it for them. [Here is a greate difference fallen **betweene the judges** of the King's Bench and my Lord Chamberleine, about the jurisdiction of their courts.[a]] Tuesday last Mr. Burton was degraded of his ministerie according to the sentence of the Star Chamber. It was fully beleivd **that all the** three delinquents should have stood in the pillory this Thursdaye after the terme, but it was putt of till the daye after, **for then the** lords sitts **in the** Star Chamber about the Bishopp of Lincolne's charges: my next letter must mention more of these **three delinquents.** I heare **my** Lord **Martiall** and my Lord of Holland both made their requests to his Majestie upon Sunday last, that since there **was soe** litle hope to **recover** the **Palatinate by** treaties that liberty might be given to his Majestie's subjects **to** send out shipps to **annoye the** Spaniard in the West Indies, **it** being graunted that the Emperour receaved all supplies to inable him to **make** warr and oppresse the Prince Elector Palatine. **It is** said **the Kinge** did soe well approve of **this** mocion as hee did promise **to adventure** sixteen **of his owne shipps in** any designe that should tend that waye; all **this I heare** reported with **some** confidence. I wrote the common **report of the** towne of the

[a] This passage has been struck out.

busines betweene the judges of the King's Bench and my Lord Chamberleine. The report of the Court is this, that Mr. Herbert the Queene's Attorney and the Recorder of London were at the boord to justifie my Lord Chamberleine's proceedings; that the Kinge usd both my Lord Chamberleine and all the judges extreamely well, saying hee would heare that difference himselfe in Michaelmas terme. The States armye is shipt, are lyeing, some neere Bergenopzome and some at the Ramekins Castle by Vlushing. The Prince of Orange drawes dayly more forces out of the garrisons and takes upp more shipps, the Prince himselfe being expected some daies since at Middleborrow, if his gowte, of which hee hath bine very lately sicke, doe not hinder him. The French continue still in Artoyes and Henolt, and beseidge Landershee,[a] in Henolt, which towne they hope to take very quickly. Hermenstaine Castle houlds out still; the commaunder is a Hugonott; if the French King's commaunder of Coblintz had bine so to, it is said that towne might have held still for the French, as the castle over against it doth. The Spaniards goe on with their forts at Gravelyn, all the other late reports of the deserting those works being contradicted by some late letters and passingers thence relate.

June 29th, 1637.

[State Papers, Domestic, ccclxii. 42.]

Fridaye last Doctor Bastwicke, Mr. Burton, and Mr. Prin stood in the pillorye in the pallace of Westminster. As Doctor Bastwicke came from the gatehouse towards the pallace the light common people strowed herbes and flowers before him; Prin and hee stood uppon one scaffold and Mr. Burton upon an other by himselfe. They all three talkt to the people; Bastwicke said they had

[a] Landrecies.

coller daies in the King's Court, and this was his coller **daye in the** King's Pallace; he was pleasant and witty all the tyme. **Prin pro**tested his inocency to the people of what was laid to his **charge.** Mr. Burton said, it was the happiest pulpett hee had ever preacht in. After twoe howers the haingman began to cutt of their eares; hee began with Mr. Burton's. There were very many people; they **wept and** greivd much for Mr. **Burton, and at the** cutting of each **eare there** was such a roareing as if every one **of** them had at the same instant lost an eare. Bastwicke gave the haingman **a knife,** and taught him to cutt of his eares quickly **and** very close, **that** hee might come there noe more. The haingman burnt Prin **in** both the cheekes, and, as I heare, because hee burnt one **cheeke** with a letter the wronge waye, hee burnt that againe; presently a surgeon clapt on a plaster to take out the fire. **The** haingman hewed off Prin's eares very scurvily, which **putt him to much** paine, and after hee stood longe in the pillorye **before his head** could be gott out, but that was a chance; the reason why Prin was soe ill usd by the haingman was hee had promisd him five peeces to use him kindly the tyme before, which he did, and Prin had given him but halfe a crowne, in five six pences; but nowe the haingman was quitt with him, for it is said **that Prin faynted in** the pillorye after the execution; **the** cause was his **standing. in the** pillorye soe long after. The humours of **the people were various,** some wept, some laught, and some were verie reservd. I heare of a popesh fellowe that told some of those which wept that if soe bee they would turne Catholiques they neede feare none of this **punishment.** Saterdaye all the towne was full of it that Mr. Prin was dead, found dead uppon his knees with his hands lift upp to heaven, but there was **noe** such thing, for I heare **hee was not** sicke. I doe **heare** the Kinge declard himselfe **to the Prince** Elector a litle before his goeing that but for **his busines he was the** happiest Kinge or Prince **in** all Christendome, **which is** most true. In my Lord Grace's speech, which is **nowe in** print, his Grace does take notice **in** his epistle to his Majestie of some reports spread abroade that the Bishopps doe **keepe** courts in their owne names, and sending abroade citations under their owne scales of armes, which these reports give out is contrary to the statute **lawe of the** land, whereby the King's prerogative is not onely violated, but **the** subject's liberty incroacht uppon. That by these rumours the subjects does often precipitate himselfe into greater inconveniences **than** he would otherwaies doe, if hee were certainely informd. The Bishopps did noe more then the lawes of the land did warrant them, and therefore his Grace does professe, **in** his foresaid speech, hee will bee an humble suitor to his Majestie that hee will require the opinion of the reverend Judges, whether their keepeing courts in their owne names as aforesaid bee not according to the lawe of the land. I heare all the Judges have mett about it, and that they have concluded the Bishopps have noe whitt incroacht uppon the King's prerogative or the subject's liberties; that eleven of the twelve Judges have subscribd yt, the other Judge haveing alsoe concented, but by reason of his absence hee hath not yet subscribd yt. It is said there shall a proclamacion bee publisht, **that** all the kingdome maye take notice of it, that the subject maye be more conformable hereafter to the Bishopp's courts. Sundaye last my Lord Stanhopp petitiond his Majestie for some reward to bee given him for resigneing his Postmaster's office **into his Ma**jesty's hands, which hee setts downe in his petitione hee did full sorely against his will. I doe not heare that hee hath any reward **given him** yet, or what **aunsweare his** Majestie hath made to this petition. Saterdaye last Sir Henry Martyn, Judge of the Admiralty, gave sentence **in a** cause betweene a Genose merchant and Captaine Walter Steward (that was in Spaine the last yeare in one of the King's shipps), **that** the Captain should paie the merchant 4000^{li}. Fridaye last **the** King's councell made an end of chargeing the Bishopp of Lincolne. Mundaye the Bishopp began his **defences.** His councell indeavourd to overthrowe **the** charges of **the bill by** logicke. It was a scholler-like defence, **and** not lawyer-like, out **of** Mr. Recorder's way, **therefore** supposd to bee of the

Bishopp's owne contriveing, but it prevaild nothing, for the court settled all the charges against the Bishopp to be legall. Tuesdaye the court sate againe. This daye the Bishopp wrote to my Lord's Grace that hee would bee pleasd to give waye that the clarke of the **peace's deposition** might bee read, which **the** judges had **subprest as** scandalous, **by reason his Grace** and Mr. Secretarie **Windebancke were** both namd in **yt.** The Bishopp desired this deposition might be read and their names left out, and to the same purpose hee prefers a petition to the **Lords of the Star Chamber** with his owne hand, which petition was first read in the inner Star Chamber and afterwards in **the** court, where alsoe his Grace caused to be **read soe much of** the Bishopp of Lincolne's letter as concernd that busines; but still all the lords denyed **the publique** reading of that deposition. Here his Grace tooke **an occasion to** cleere himselfe of Mr. Kylvert's acquaintance. **The deposition was** that Mr. Kylvert would have perswaded the clarke **of the** peace to have swoarne thus and thus against the Bishopp, which hee said hee would not doe with a safe conscience. Saith Kylvert againe, if it bee true what you sware, what should you feare? if it bee not, yet my Lord's Grace of Canterbury and Mr. Secretarie Windebancke shall give you thancks for yt. My **Lord's Grace declard** untill such a tyme **(which** was after this deposition **taken)** hee knewe not Mr. Kylvert's face; the **first tyme** of seeing **him being** behind the King's counsell **in that court,** one of their lordships that **sate next to** him shewing him Kylvert; and that hee had never **spoake to** him but once, which was the last sommer, **when** hee **movd him to** bestowe a liveing upon a poore parson, which liveing I told Kylvert the **Kinge had** given three weekes before: **and to** all this **his Grace tendered** his oath; and therefore, **why Mr.** Kylvert should **abuse him** thus he knewe not, **but therefore desired,** as in like things concerneing himself, all petitions **and** depositions might bee publiquely read, which the **court still** disallowed, yet I heare all their lordships tooke notice of **this** deposition in the Star Chamber. Wensdaye some depositions **were read to prove** howe

Mr. Kylvert had provockt the Bishopp of **Lincolne** at a Commission held at Lincolne, upon which the Bishopp did call Kylvert many bace **names**, which is a charge in his bill against **the** Bishopp. The **Bishopp's counsell** prest these depositions soe **home** that my Lord**'s Grace said**, wee are fully satisfied in court that Mr. Kylvert **did** misbehave himselfe to the Bishopp, therefore lett us goe to **some other charge**, which cutts Mr. Kylvert from his dammages, which he hopt the **court** would have given him. One thing Mr. Recorder said this daye, which was, that it was not possible to wash the Bishopp cleare **of** his private tampering with witnesses, for severall men deposd severally against the Bishopp for tampering with them; but in all other things wherein these men were in question **the** depositions provd them faulty, and therefore hee hopt their Lordships would take that into their considerations, and give noe creditt **to their** depositions against the Bishopps. There is somewhat **of** Sir John Moonson which I cannot yet learn; my next **letter shall** have it, **for** I must set downe punctually what concernes **the creditt** of other men of speaciall note. Fridaye the Bishopp **makes an** end of his **defences.** As Mr. Prin returnd from his **execution** to the Tower **hee** made these verses. S. L. Lauds Scars:

    Triumphant I returne, my face discryes
      Laud's scorching Scarrs,
    God's gratefull sacrifice.
    S. L. Stigmata Laudis.
    Stigmata maxellis baiulans insignia Laudis
    Exultans remeo victima grata Deo.

July 6th, 1637

[State Papers, Domestic, ccclxiii. 119.]

July 13, 1637.

The Lords have sent a commaund to the Star Chamber Office to drawe upp the order to send Doctor **Bastwicke**, Mr. Burton, and Mr. Prin to their severall remote prisons. The letters are already provided to bee sent to the high sheriffs of those counties to take them into their custody and to observe the decree of the court, which is, that they keepe from them pen, inke, and paper, and all bookes, save onely the Bible and the Booke of Common Prayer, and some other bookes of devotion, such as shall be allowed them. There is a report abroade in the towne that the Minister of Shoreditch, observeing the humours of the people soe much to compassionate these three delinquents, should deliver in his sermon that they all incurrd damnation which thought well of those three, whoe had bine justly punisht for their demeritts. This doctrine made divers goe out of the church, for the common people are extreamely compassionate towards them. One Doctor Layton was punisht in the pillorye about seven yeares since for the like offences against the Bishopps, and hath layen in the Fleete ever since; by an order of the last weeke hee is also to be removd to some remote prison. Fridaye last my Lord Moone's sonne was committed prisoner to the Fleete for drawing his swoard uppon Ludgate Hill and hurteing my Lord Lomely, whoe sate quietly in his coach, there being a stopp of coaches, Mr. Moone's coach was amonge them; hee supposd himselfe wrongd by some, drewe his swoard and strooke them which were next him, for which hee is not onely committed but his Majestie since being acquainted with yt hath ordered that Mr. Attorney shall putt an informacion into the Star Chamber against him. That deposition concerning Sir John

* Parson Catlyn, a most abominable rogue, taken a bed with three whores at once, but deprived for being commonly druncke when he did administer the Sacrament.

Moonson which I promisd in my last was thus: Parson Catlyn deposeth for the Bishopp of Lincolne, that hee mett one Parkinson, Mr. Amcott's servant, at the Balye in Lincolne, and askt him what hee made there; said Parkinson, I am come hether to swoare against the Bishopp of Lincolne. Sir John Moonson hath given mee a some of money to sweare lustily, and I will feather my nest soe longe as I live. This is Catlyn's deposition. To overthrowe this, Parkinson is clad in a parson's habite and brought into Catlyn's company and presented to Catlyn under the name of Parson Watkins, of Yorkshire; nowe, it is said, if Catlyn had not knowne him, as affedavitts would have bine made to that purpose, the consequence would have bine hee must needes have forswearne himselfe in deposeing hee heard Parkinson saye (as aforesaid), this Catlyn not knoweing Parkinson; but Catlyn did knowe him, and cald him by his name, although Parkinson denyed himselfe at the first; alsoe some depositions were that Parkinson had upon him those very cloathes which Sir John Moonson's chapleine read prayers in in Sir John Moonson's house. Fridaye and Saturdaye last Mr. Attorney made his reply, wherein hee multiplyes the Bishopp's offences, as if soe bee the Bishopp's councell had washt off none of those charges. Hee shewes his Majesty's zeale to maintaine his lawes, that rather then hee will suffer his lawes to be violated hee will not spare to call in question any of his greate lords, meaneing in this cause the Bishopp of Lincolne, whoe had borne the greatest office of the kingdome. In Mr. Attorney's replye hee causeth some depositions to be read to cleare that pretended plott of the disguiseing Parkinson in a preist's habite, it being deposd that Parkinson haveing of his owne meere mocion putt himselfe into blacke, Sir John Moonson's man jestingly led him into Parson Catlyn's company by the waye of mirth, and not uppon any plott, as was pretended in those depositions taken for the Bishopps The Attorney did presse their Lordships to give Sir John Moonson good dammages for those aspertions the Bishopp of

Lincolne had cast uppon him. Alsoe hee desired their Lordships to take it in their considerations that there were some presidents, which hee named, where Bishopps had bine deprivd for lesse offences then the Bishopp of Lincolne was now fully provd to bee guilty of, therefore hee besought their Lordships first to fine the Bishopp and then to remitt him to the High Commission to bee there deprivd of all his spirituall promotions, being nowe unworthy to hold any of them. The same Saterdaye the Bishopp of Lincolne went to Greenewich to make use of all his helpes to take of the sentence which the lords had appointed to bee the Tuesdaye followeing. Hee procured my Lord Duke[a] to preferr his petition, which hee did; besides hee usd all the arguments hee could to perswade his Majestie to take the Bishopp to his mercy. The Kinge told my Lord Duke hee would returne noe aunsweare till after the sentence was pronounost against him. The Bishopp of Lincolne did not rest here, but prevaild soe much as some above the Duke movd the Kinge in his behalfe, but it might not prevaild; I heare the Bishopp proffered largely. Tuesday the lords mett in the Star Chamber before they came into the court; they sate councell neere twoe howers in the Inner Chamber after they came into court, where my Lord Cottington began the sentence. His Lordshipe tooke it that the charge against the Bishopp for subornation was fully provd against him; all the lords were of that opinion, that severall subornations were provd besides divers other fowle misdemeanours; my Lord Cottington's sentence was ten thousand pounds fine to the Kinge, imprisonment in the Tower durcing the King's pleasure, to bee remitted to the High Commission, there to bee suspended *ab officijs et beneficijs*, if the Kinge soe please; and 1000 markes dammages to Sir John Moonson, whome all their Lordships did commend to have discreectely demeand himselfe in the whole progresse of this busines. All the lords concurred in this sentence, soe that there was neither degradation nor depriva-

---

[a] The Duke of Lennox.

tion as was talkt of before; most of their Lordships did agree that
Mr. Kylvert had much misbehavd himselfe towards the Bishopp,
onely my Lord's Grace, hee would not approve of all hee did, yet
hee commended Mr. Kylvert's courage in prosecuteing the **cause,**
saying, the King's cause must needes have suffered if it had bine
prosecuted with lesse spirite, considering the Bishopp's potencie in
the countrie. The Archbishopp compard Parson Catlyn to Catelyn,
that arch traytor of Roome, for it was provd that this Parson Catlyn
had swoarne to a blancke in the behalfe of the Bishopp of Lincolne,
whoe was to have given him a good liveing, besides some other
fowle things provd against Catlyn. Alsoe there were some depo-
sitions that the Bishopp said it had cost him a 1000^{li} at one commission held **at** Lincolne, which their Lordships concluded hee
could not spend but by corrupted and suborneing of witnesses; the
judges concluded to[a] **practice to** subornation and subornation itselfe
were all one, and deservd equall punishment. My Lord's Grace
shewed first what hee had done on behalfe of the Bishopp to take
him off from this prosecution; that hee had movd his Majestie five
times for him upon his knees; that hee had prevaild more for him
then all the other meanes hee had made; that his Majestie alwayes
askt him if the Bishopp would submitt and acknowledge **his errors;**
that hee had subscribd the King's aunsweare to the Bishopp's peti-
tion with his owne hand (which hee did not nowe commend him-
selfe for, since the Bishopp was soe guilty of subornation); that
the Bishopp had acknowledgd his favours by letters under his owne
hand, which his Grace said hee had yet to shewe; yet, said his
Grace, hath the Bishopp bine most extreamely ingratefull towards
him; my Lord's Grace hightens the Bishopp's offences of subornation out of devine **and** humane writt, soe agreed with my Lord
Cottington. Lord Privey Seale began thus, that hee had knowne
many servants had undone themselves to uphold the creditt of their
masters, but till now he never knewe any master undone to uphold

[a] ? that.

the creditt of his servant; this was my Lord of Lincolne's case in his upholding the creditt of Prydean, whoe was accusd for getting a bastard, and the Bishopp would cleare him of it. My Lord Keeper, though hee cleard the Bishopp of many things for which the other lords did fine him, yet hee said the Bishopp did *Ludere Periurijs*, which was the sharpest sensure given him; but the lords, many of them did professe three severall subornations were fully provd against him. It was ordered that daye that the first bill against the Bishopp of Lincolne should bee sett downe for heareing the next tearme. And this was the sentence. One passage more of my Lord Grace's in agravation of subornation, that this sinn was longe conceald, all the tyme before the lawe, and some ages after the lawe of Moses was delivered the Holy Ghost would not prompt nature to it by a prohibition of it. His Grace said, that, to his remembrance, Jezabell was the first suborner of falce wittnesses; this wee might gather out of the text yett somewhat obscurely sett downe. Tuesdaye last my Lord Russell was married to my Lady Ann Carr. They were married with all the privacie that might bee. They kept their marriadge at Mr. Carr's house, right against the Busse[a] in the Strand; it was soe private as there was very litle notice taken of it.

July this 13th, 1637.

[a] Britain's Burse.

VII.

THE WILL OF WILLIAM PRYNN.

[Registry of the Prerogative Court of Canterbury.]

In the name of God Amen. I, William Prynne of Lyncolnes Inne, in the county of Middlesex, esquire, being, through God's mercy, restored to perfect health and of sound memory from my late infirmitie (for which I bless his holy name), considering my owne declyning strength, the deathes of many of my relacions younger then myselfe, and my approaching dissolucion, being willing to be dissolved and to be with Chryst which is best of all, whenever God shall please to take me out of this vayne and wicked world, and hath noe more worke for me therein, doe make this my last will and testament in forme ensueing: First, I bequeathe my immortall soule into the hands of God frome whome I receaved it, by whose free grace, and all-satisfactory merritts of my Lord and Saviour Jesus Christ, I stedfastly hope and beleeve to obtayne the full pardon of all my sinnes and eternall life in his heavenly kingdome. My vile body I bequeath to the dust, to be decently interred in the parish church of Swanswicke, in the county of Sommersett, or Lyncolnes Inne, if I decease in or nere either of them, till God shall raise it up a glorious body, and reunite it for ever to my soule at the general resurrection. Item, I give and bequeath to the Churchwardens and Treasurers of Christ Church in London, towards the repairing thereof, the summe of tenne pounds; and to the Churchwardens and Treasurers of the parish churches of Saint Antholines, Saint Lawrence neare the Guilehall, Saint Bridgett, and Saint Katherines Creed Church, defaced by the late dreadful fire, five pounds a peece, to be paid them within three monthes after they shall beginne to repaire them respectively, in case I dye before that tyme, haveing already given the somme of tenne pounds a peece to the Treasurers of Saint Maryes Aldermanbury and Sepulchers, and five pounds to the Churchwardens of Saint Mildred's, with my owne handes, to bee imployed only on the repaires of the saide churches, and for noe other uses. Item, I give to the library of Lyncolnes Inn all my manuscripts of Parlyament Rolles and Journalls, and other records not yet published, together with my Rerum Germanicarum Scriptores in five,[a] Rerum Hispanicarum Scriptores in four, and Goldastus in three folio volumes. Item, I give to the Library of Oriel Colledge, in Oxford, whereof I was both a member and tennant, my Ocham upon the Sentences, Saint Briget's Revellacions,[b] Laurentius Surius his Councils in four tomes, and one of each sort of my owne printed bookes which they yet want. All the rest of my divinity and ecclesiasticall history bookes I give to my dear brother, Mr. Thomas Prynne, and all my other history bookes, phisick, philosophy, chirurgery bookes, and poets I give to my nephew William Clerke, with this proviso, that he shall not sell them. And for my law bookes I give soe many of them to my brother George Clerke as he shall make choyce of. Item, I give to my dear brother, Mr. Thomas Prynne, my best gold ringe with my father's armes, and three old peeces of gold which were my grandfather's. Item, I give to my dear sister, Mistresse Katheryne Clerke, my best serjeant's ring, all

---

[a] The books given to Lincoln's Inn are not indicated in the library of that Society as having been the subjects of this bequest, but several of the manuscripts in that library have Prynne's handwriting in them, or can be shown in other ways to have passed through his hands. [This and the following note are in Mr. Bruce's hand.]

[b] These books do not appear in Coxe's Catalogue of the MSS. in the library of Oriel College, nor is Prynne reckoned among the benefactors of the library of that College.

my hangings, bedding, furniture in my chamber in Lyncolnes Inne, and two hundred pounds in money. Item, I give to her husband, Mr. George Clerke, one of my gold rings. Item, I give to every one of their sonnes and daughters who shall be living at the tyme of my decease one gold ring and one hundred pounds a peece. And to my neece Elizabeth Clerke and her daughter Elizabeth one gold ring and tenne pounds a peece in plate. Item, I give to my disconsolate neece, Mrs. Catherine Colman, widow, the somme of two hundred poundes in money; to each of her daughters the somme of one hundred pounds; and to her sonnes the sum of fiftie poundes, provided that if either her daughters dye or her sons before marriage his or her portion shall remayne to the surviving daughter. Item, I give to my neece Collett, my neece Browne, and my neece ([a]) forty pounds a peece. And to each of their respective children tenne pounds a peece. And in case any of their respective children shall dye before marriage, that the legacie of the deceased shall remayne to the survivor. Item, I give to my cousin Joyce Prynne the somme of 30^{li}, and to my neece Becke her sister the like somme, if alive at my decease. Item, I give to my clerke Ralph Jennings one of my cloth suites, with a coate, cloake, stockings, and hatt, with five poundes in money, to be paid to him by 5^s each weeke, lest he spend or be cheated thereof. Item, I give to my clerke Samuell Wiseman the somme of three pounds and one of my silk cloakes and last printed bookes. Item, I give to Doctor Tilletson one of each of my three tomes of my Exact Chronologicall Vindicacion, 8vo. bound. Item, I give and bequeath to the Churchwardens and Overseers of the Poore of the parish of Swanswicke the somme of tenne pounds, to be imployed in binding forth poore boyes and girles therein apprentices as my nephew Mr. George Clerke and the Minister of the parish shall nominate and directe. Item, I give to Thomas Smith, of Swanswick, the somme of twenty shillings in money and

---

[a] "Non est legibile" is written in the margin of the copy from which this is printed.

one of my suites of apparell and riding coates. Item, I give to my brother George Clarke all the bedding and furniture of my chamber in the Tower of London. Item, I give to Mr. William Ryley one of my last tomes of a Chronologicall Vindicacion. All the legacies in money formerly given I desire may be paid with all expedicion out of the sale and proceed of my printed books at my owne charge in my chamber and elsewhere, and of six yeares and half arreares of my annuall sallary and fee of **five hundred** pounds, as Keeper of the Records of the Tower, freely given mee by his Majesty King Charles the Second of his owne meere motion, for my services and sufferings for him under the late usurpers, and strenuous endeavours, by printing and otherwise, to restore his Majestie to the actuall possession of his royall government and kingdome without opposicion or effusion of blood. As for my interest in the lease of Swanswick, and my hangings, pictures, and furniture there, I give and bequeath them to my dear brother, Mr. Thomas Prynne, for the use of my beloved sister, Mrs. Katherine Clerke, for her better mayntenance dureing her naturall life. And if she dye before the expiracion of the said terme, then to the use of her husband and my nephew, George Clerk, if living. All the rest of my reall and personall estate, goods, chattels, debts, creditts (I never coveting the uncertaine transient treasures, honors, or preferments of this world, but to doe my God, King, country all the best publicke services I could with the losse of my liberty, expences of my meane estate, and hazard of my life) I give and bequeath to my deare brother, Mr. Thomas Prynne, and my loveing sister, Mrs. Katharine Clerke, whom I make sole executors of this my last will and testament, revoking all former wills. In testimony whereof I have written it with my owne hand, and sealed and signed it with my owne seale of armes and hand this eleventh day of August, in the yeare of our Lord 1669.

WILLIAM PRYNNE.

Signed, sealed, published, and declared by the testator to be his very last will and testament, in the presence of THOMAS PRYNNE.

Probatum fuit testamentum suprascriptum apud ædes Exoinenses[a] scituat. in le Strand, in cona.[b] Middx. coram venerabili viro Timotheo Baldwyn, **Legum** Doctore Surrogato, venerabilis et egregij viri Leolinj Jenkins, Curiæ Prerogativæ Cantuarensis mag'ri Custodis sive Commissarij l'time constituto vicessimo quinto die mensis Novembris, anno Domini Mill[es]imo sexcentesimo sexagesimo nono Juramentis Thomas Prynne et **Catherina Clerke executorum in** hujismodi Testamento nomınat. quibus commissa. fuit administracio omnium et singulorum bonorum jurium et creditorum dicti defuncti de bene et fidelr administrand' **eadem** ad Sancta Dei Evangelia jurat.

      Tнos. Dyneley,
      John Iggulden, } Deputy Registers.
      W. F. Gostling,

[a] *Sic.*   [b] *Sic* for Com.

APPENDIX.

LIST OF PRYNNE'S WORKS BY J. BRUCE.

The Perpetuitie of a Regenerate Man's Estate. 4to. [1627].
> Without title-page. Commences with address "To all those of Church of England * * slaunder the Patrons of the * * final perseverance of the Saints."
> The body of the book contains pp. 410. This seems to be the first edition.

The perpetuitie of a regenerate man's Estate. The second Edition perused and inlarged. London. 4to. 1627.
> Besides the prefatory address in the first edition there are in this edition addresses to Archbishop Abbot and to the Christian Reader, and the book contains pp. 548.

The Vnlouelinesse of Love Lockes, or a Svmmarie Discovrse prooning: The wearing, and nourishing of a Locke, or Loue-Locke, to be altogether vnseemely, and vnlawfull vnto Christians. London. 4to. 1628.

A Briefe Svrvay and Censvre of Mr. Cozens his couzening Deuotions. London. 4to. 1628.

Healthes Sicknesse; or a compendious and briefe discourse prouing the drinking and pledging of Healthes to be sinfull and vtterly vnlawfull vnto Christians. London. 4to. 1628.

The Church of England's old Antithesis to new Arminianisme. London. 4to. 1629.
> Annexed to the present publication is,—

God no Impostor nor Deluder. 4to. 1629.

Anti-Arminianism: or the Church of England's old Antithesis to new Arminianism, &c. Lond. 1630.
> It was twice printed that year in 4to. [Bodl. B. 24, 2 Linc.] Wood, iii. 855.

Lame Giles his Haultings, together with an Appendix concerning the

Popish Original and Progress of Bowing at the Name of Jesus. Lond. 1631. 4to.

Histrio-Mastix. The Players Scourge or Actor's Tragœdie. Lond. Michael Sparke. 4to. 1633.

Appendix, Supplementum, & Epilogus, ad Flagellum Pontificis: touching the Parity of Bishops and Presbyters Jure devino. An. 1635.

A Breviate of the Bishops' intolerable Usurpations and Encroachments upon the King's Prerogative, and Subjects' Liberties; with an Appendix to it. 1635.

Certain Queries propounded to the Bowers at the Name of Jesus, and the Patrons thereof. 1636.

The unbishoping of Timothy and Titus. London. 4to. 1636. Reprint of 1660.

A divine Tragedy lately acted : or a Collection of sundry memorable Examples of God's Judgment upon Sabbath-breakers, &c. 1636. 4to.

 Printed by stealth.

News from Ipswich, discovering certain late detestable Practices of some domineering lordly Prelates, to undermine the established Doctrine and Discipline of our Church, &c. 1636. 4to.

 Printed in one sheet, published under the name of Matthew White three times in 1636, and another time in 1641.

Instructions for Church-Wardens concerning Visitation-Articles, Fees, Oathes, &c. 1636.

Certain Queries propounded to Bishops, &c. 1636.

Looking-Glass for all Lordly Prelates. 1636.

Additions to the first Part of a Dialogue between A. and B. concerning the Sabbath's Morality, and the Unlawfulness of Pastimes on the Lord's Day.

 Twice printed in 1636.

A Breviate of the Prelates intolerable usurpations. Published by W. Huntley. 3rd Edition. 4to. 1637.

 8 is No. 2, 8 a is 1. No. 1 has some additional matter at the end. It is in the vol. lettered " Huntley and Prynne ag^t the Bps." [a]

[a] This seems to refer to copies in Mr. Bruce's possession.

Catalogue of such Testimonies in all Ages, as plainly evidence Bishops and Presbyters to be both one, equal and the same in Jurisdiction, Office, &c. by divine Law and Institution, &c. 1637.

> Reprinted in 4to. in double columns, 1641.

A quench Coal, with an Appendix to it, in Answer to A Coal from the Altar, and other Pamphlets, touching Altars, and bowing to, or towards, them. 1637.

A Breife Relation of certaine speciall, and most materiall passages, and speeches in the Starre-Chamber, occasioned and delivered June the 14th, 1637, at the Censure of those three worthy Gentlemen, Dr. Bastwicke, Mr. Burton, and Mr. Prynne. 4to. 1638.

Woodstreet-Compter's Plea for its Prisoner: Or the sixteen Reasons which induce Nathan. Wickins, late Servant to Mr. Will. Prynne, but now Prisoner in the said Compter, to refuse to take the Oath ex officio, wherein, &c. 1638. 4to.

> Printed in ten sheets, published under the name of Nath. Wickins; yet it was generally supposed that Prynne was the chief composer because of the many quotations therein.

Lord Bishops none of the Lord's Bishops. Nov. 1640. 4to.

Petition to be recalled from Exile, &c. 1640.

Mount-Orgueil: or divine and profitable Meditations raised from the Contemplations of these three Leaves of Nature's Volume. 1. Rocks. 2. Seas. 3. Gardens. Lond. 1641. 4to.

A Poetical Description of Mount-Orgueil Castle in the Isle of Jersey. Lond. 1641. 4to.

The Soules Complaint against the Bodies Encroachments on her. London. Michael Sparke. 4to. 1641.

Pleasant Purge for a Roman Catholic to evacuate his evil Humours, consisting of a Century of polemical Epigrams. Lond. 1641. 4to.

The Antipathie of the English Lordly Prelacie both to Regall Monarchy, and Civill Unity. The First and Second Part. London. 4to. Michael Sparke. 1641.

The Antipathie of the English Lordly Prelacie both to Regall Monarchy and Civill Unity. The first Part. London. Michael Sparke. 4to. 1641.

A New Discovery of the Prelates Tyranny, in the prosecutions of Prynne, Burton, and Bastwick. London, for M. S. 4to. 1641.
> No. 1, with portraits of Prynne, Burton, and Bastwick (lettered Huntley, &c.). No. 2 is without the portraits (duplicates). No. 3 has a portrait of Laud as well as the others.

A terrible Out-cry against the **loytering** exhalted Prelates: shewing the Danger and Unfitness of conferring them in any temporal Office or Dignity, &c. Lond. 1641. **4to**.
> Not Prynne's book, though his name be to it.

A Christian Sea-Card. London. Michael Sparke. 4to. 1641.

A Christian Paradise. London Michael Sparke. 4to. 1641.

Rockes Improved. London. Michael Sparke. 4to. 1641.

A Soveraigne Antidote to prevent, Appease, and Determine our Unnaturall and Destructive Civill Wars and Dissentions. Also *Vox Popvli*. 1st Edition. London. Richard Lownds. 4to. 1642.

A Soveraign Antidote to prevent, appease, and determine our unnatural and destructive Civil Warres and dissentions. London. 2nd Edition. 4to. 1642.

Vindication of Psal. 105, ver. 15, (Touch not my anointed and do my Prophets no harm) from some false Glosses lately obtruded on by Priests and Royalists. Lond. 1642.
> And 44 in one sheet, in 4to.

A Catalogue of printed Books written by William Prynne, &c. before, during, since, his Imprisonment. Lond. Mich. Sparke, sen^r. 4to. 1643.
> With Sparke, the stationer's, preface.

The Treachery and Disloyalty of Papists to their Soveraigns, with the Soveraign Power of Parliaments and Kingdoms, in 4 Parts. Lond. 1643. Large 4to.
> First edition.

The Soveraigne Power of Parliaments and Kingdomes. In foure parts, with Appendix. (2nd Edition of part I.) London. Michael Sparke. 4to. 1643.

An humble Remonstrance against the Tax of **Ship-Money**. London. Michael Sparke. 4to. **1643**.
  Written 1636; corruptly printed 1641. Wood, iii. 855.

Romes Master-Peece. 1st Edition. London. Michael Sparke. 4to. 1643.

The Opening of **the Great** Seale of England. **London**. Michael Sparke. **4to. 1643.**

The Popish Royal Favourite. London. Michael Sparke. **4to.** 1643.

The Doome of Cowardize and Treachery. London. **Michael** Sparke. **4to. 1643.**

The Doome of Cowardisze **and Treachery.** Lond. Michael Sparke. 4to. **1643.**

A Breviate of the Life of William Laud, archbishop **of Canterbury.** Lond. fol. Michael Sparke. **1644.**

Romes Master-Peece. 2nd Edition. London. **Michael Sparke. 4to.** 1644.

Moderate Apology against a pretended Calumny: in Answer to some Passages in The Preheminence of Parliaments, published by James Howell, &c. In one sheet. **Lond.** 1644. 4to.

Check to Britannicus for his palpable Flattery, &c. Lond. 1644.

The Falsities **and Forgeries** of the Anonymous Author of **a** Pamphlet entitled **The Fallacies of** Mr. Will. Prynne, discovered in a short View of his Book intit. The Sovereignty of Parliaments. 1644.

Four Serious Questions touching Excommunication and Suspension from the Sacrament. **Lond. 1644. 4to.**

Twelve considerable Questions touching Church-government "(sadly **propounded out** of a real Desire of Unity and Tranquility in Church **and State) to all** sober minded Christians," &c. Lond. **1644.** 4to.

Independency Examined, unmasked, refuted. By **twelve** new particular interrogatories. London. F. L. for Michael **Sparke.** 4to. 1644.

A full **Reply to** certain brief **Observations** and Anti-queries on **Mr.**

CAMD. SOC.   P

Prynne's 12 Questions about Church-government, &c. Lond. 1644. 4to.

Brief Animadversions on Mr. John Goodwin's Theomachia, &c. **Lond.** 1644. 4to.

A True Relation of the Prosecution of Colonel Nathaniel **Fiennes.** London. Michael Sparke. 4to. **1644.**

Just Defence of John Bastwick, **Dr. of Physic,** against the Calumnies of John Lilbourne, Lieutenant **Col. and** his false Accusations : written in Way of Reply to **a Letter of Mr. Vickars,** &c. Lond. 1645. 4to.

The Lyar confounded, or **a** brief Refutation of Joh. Lilbourne's miserably **mis-stated** Case, mistaken, **&c. against the** high **Court of Parliament, &c.** The honourable Committee of Examinations, &c. Lond. 1645. 4to.

Truth triumphing over **Falsehood,** Antiquity over Novelty : **or a seasonable** Vindication **of the undoubted ecclesiastical** Jurisdiction, Right, Legislative, and Coercive Power **of** Christian Emperors, &c. in matter of religion, &c. in Refutation of John Goodwin's Innocencies Triumph, and his dear brother Burton's Vindication of Churches commonly called Independent, &c. Lond. 1645. 4to.

Hidden **Workes** of **Darkenes** brought to Publike Light. **Lond.** Michael Sparke. **Fol. 1645.**

Suspention suspended. **London. Michael** Sparke. **4to. 1646.**

A Vindication of four Questions, concerning Excommunication and Suspension from the **Lord's** Supper. London. Michael Sparke. 4to. 1645.

Fresh Discovery of **some** prodigious new wandring blazing Stars and Firebrands, stiling themselves New Lights, firing our Church **and State** into new **Combustions.** Divided into 10 Sections, comprising &c. Lond. 1646. 4to. **To which** are added, of **Prynne's** collection, Letters, Papers, and a Petition lately sent from the Summer **Islands** touching the schismatical, illegal, tyrannical Proceedings of some Independents **there,** &c.

Diotrephes Catechised. London. Michael Sparke. **4to.** 1646.

Twelve Questions of public Concernment, touching **the Regulation of** some Abuses in the Law and Legal Proceedings. Lond. **1646.** 4to.

Scotland's ancient Obligation to England and public Acknowledgment thereof **for their** brotherly Assistance and Deliverance of them. Lond. 1646. 4to.

Scotland's public Acknowledgment of God's just Judgments upon their Nation for their frequent Breach of Faiths, Leagues, Oaths, &c. Lond. 1646. 4to.

Canterburies Doome, or the first part of a compleat History of the Commitment, Charge, Tryall, Condemnation, Execution of William Laud, Late Arch-Bishop of Canterbury. London. Michael Spark. Fol. 1646.

Minors no Senators. Lond. 1646. 4to.

A Gag for long-hair'd Rattle-heads. Lond. 1646. 4to.

Plaine and short Expedient to settle the Distractions of the Kingdom. Lond. 1647.

Counter-plea to the Coward's Apology. Lond. 1647.

Account of the King's Majesty's Revenues and Debts. Lond. 1647.

Declaration of the Officer's and Armie's illegal injurious Proceedings **and** Practices against **the** 11 **impeached** Members. Lond. 1647.

Eight Queries **upon the** Declaration, and late Letter of the Army. Lond. **1647.**

Nine Queries upon the printed Charge of the Army against the 11 Members. Lond. 1647.

The Hypocrites unmask'd. London. 1647.

New Presbyterian Light, springing out of Independent Darkness. **Lond.** 1647.

The total and final Demands of the Army. Lond. 1647.

Brief Justification of the 11 accused Members from a scandalous Libel. Lond. 1647.

The Levellers levell'd, &c. **Lond. 1647.**

APPENDIX.

The Sword of Christian Magistracy Supported; or a full Vindication of Christian Kings and Magistrates Authority under the Gospell to punish Idolatry, Apostacy, &c. London. for John Bellamie. 4to. 1647.

Vindication of Sir Will. Lewes from his Charge. Lond. 1647.

Full Vindication and Answer of the 11 accused Members, viz. Denz. Hollis, &c. to a late printed pamphlet intit. A particular Charge or Impeachment in the Name of Sir Tho. Fairfax and the Army against the 11 Members. Lond. 1647. 4to.

The Lords and Commons first Love to, Zeal for, and earnest Vindication of their injuriously accused and impeached Members, and violated Privileges, &c. Lond. 1647. 4to.

The University of Oxford's Plea refuted: or a full Answer to a late printed Paper entit. The Privileges of the University of Oxford in Point of Visitation, &c. Lond. 1647. 4to.

Nine proposals by Way of Interrogation, to the General, Officers, and Soldiers of the Army, concerning the Justice of their proceedings in Law of Conscience against the Parliament. Lond. 1647. 4to.

Twelve Queries of public Concernment. Lond. 1647. 4to.

Public Declaration and solemn Protestation of the Freemen of England, against the illegal, intolerable, undoing Grievance of Free-quarter. Lond. 1648. 4to.

The Machiavillian Cromwellist. Lond. 1648.

Irenarches redevivus: or, a brief Collection of sundry useful Statutes and Petitions in Parliament (not hitherto printed) concerning the Necessity, Institution, Office, Oaths, &c. of Justices of Peace. Lond. 1648. 4to.

Ardua Regni, or XII. Arduous Doubts of great concernment to the Kingdome. 4to. 1648.

The Case of the impeached Lords, Commons, and Citizens truly stated. Lond. 1648. 4to.

Practical Law controuling, countermanding the Common Law, and the Sword of War, the Sword of Justice. Exeter 1648.

A Plea for the Lords. London. 4to. 1648.
 Another Edition. **London. 4to. 1658.**
The Petition of Right of the Freeholders and Freemen of the **Kingdom** of England. **Lond. 1648. 4to.**
A New **Magna Charta. Lond. 1648.**
The **County of Somerset divided into** several Classes. Lond. 1648.
Mercurius Rusticus, containing News from several Counties of England, and **their joynt Addresses to the Parliament. Lond. 1648.**
Just and solemn **Protestation and Remonstrance of the** Lord-Mayor, Common-Council-men, **and Freemen of Lond. Lond. 1648.**
True and perfect **Narrative of the Officers and Army's** Force upon the Common's House, and **Members. Lond. 1648.**
Second Part of the Narrative concerning the Army's Force **upon the** Common's House, and **Members.** Lond. 1648.
Protestation of **the** secured and secluded Members. **1648.**
Demand of his (Prynne's) **Liberty** to the General, **26 Dec.** 1648, with his Answer thereto, **and his** Answer and **Declaration** thereupon.
Remonstrance and Declaration of several Counties, Cities, and Boroughs, **against the** Unfaithfulness of **some** of their Knights, Citizens, and Burgesses. Lond. 1648.
Letter **to the General (sir** Thomas Fairfax), dated **3 Jan. 1648,** demanding what kind **of a Prisoner he is?** and whose Prisoner? **with an** Appearance **to his Action of false** Imprisonment. With an additional Postscript.
Impeachment of High-Treason against Lieutenant-Gen. Cromwell, and other Army Officers. Jan. **1648.**
Four considerable Positions for the sitting Members, Judges, and others to **ruminate upon.** Jan. 1648.
His Declaration **and Protestation** against the present Proceedings **of the** General **and general Council** of the Army **and their Faction, now** remaining and sitting in the said House. **19 Jan. 1648.**
Six Propositions of undoubted Verity, fit to be considered of in our present Exigency, by all **loyal** subjects **and** conscientious Christians. **4to.**

Six serious Queries concerning the **King's Tryal by the new high Court of Justice.** Lond. 1648.

Mr. Prinne's Charge against the King; shewing that the King's Design, **Purpose, and** Resolution, has always been engag'd, **byass'd,** and **tended to settle,** establish, &c. Slavery in, among, over, his Dominions, Subjects, People, &c. Lond. 1648. 4to.
    Not Prynne.

Proclamation proclaiming **Charles Pr. of Wales, King** of Gr. Britain, France, **and** Ireland, 1 **Feb. in the first year** of his Reign. 1648.

Declaration **and** Protestation **of the Peers,** Lords, **and** Barons **against** the Usurpations of **some Members of** the Common House, **8 Feb. 1648.**

Public Declaration and **Protestation of the secured** and secluded **Members** of the House **of Commons, against the** treasonable **and** illegal **late Acts** and Proceedings **of some few** Confederate **Members** of **that House,** since their forcible **Exclusion, 13** Feb. 1648.

The Substance of a Speech **made in the House of** Commons **by Wil. Pryun of** Lincolns-Inn, **Esquire ; On Munday** the Fourth **of December, 1648.** London. **Mich.** Spark. **4to.** 1649.
    Three editions came out in less than one year.

Appendix **for** the Kingdom's **better** Satisfaction of some Occurrences since **the** said Speech.
    Printed with, and **added to,** one of the editions of the said speech (4th Dec. 1648).

A Breife Memento **to the** present Vnparliamentary Junto, Touching **their** present intentions and proceedings to Depose and Execute **Charles** Stewart, **their lawful** King. London. **4to.** 1649.
    Reprinted 1660.

A Vindication of **the** Imprisoned **and** Secluded Members of the House **of** Commons. **London.** Michael **Spark.** 4to. 1649.

New Babel's Confusion : **or,** several Votes of the **Commons assembled in** Parliament, against certain Papers entit. The Agreement **of the** People, &c. **Lond.** 1649. **4to.**

Prynne the Member reconciled to Prynne **the** Barrester ; **or an Answer**

to a Scandalous Pamphlet, Intituled Prynne against Prynne. London. 4to. 1649.

First Part of **an Historical Collection of** the antient Councils **and Parliaments of England, from the** year 673, till an. 1216, &c. Lond. 1649. 4to.

A Legall Vindication of the Liberties of England against Illegall Taxes **and pretended Acts of Parliament** lately enforced **on the** People. *1st Edition*. London. Robert Hodges. 4to. **1649.**

A Legall Vindication of the Liberties of England against Illegall Taxes and pretended Acts of Parliaments. *2nd Edition*. London. Robert Hodges. 4to. 1649.

Reprinted with additions **1660.**

Summary **Reasons against the new Oath and** Engagement. And an Admonition to all such as have already subscrib'd to it, &c. **1649. 4to.**

A Serious Epistle to Mr. William Prynne. London. **4to. 1649.**

Arraignment, Conviction, and Condemnation of the **Westmonasterian** Junctoe's Engagement. **Lond. 1650. 4to.**

Brief Apology **for all Non-subscribers,** and Looking-glass for all Apostate Prescribers and Subscribers of the new Engagement. Lond. 1650. **4to.**

The Time-serving Proteus and Ambidexter Divine, uncased to the World. Lond. 1650. **4to.**

Sad and Serious Considerations touching the invasive War against our Presbyterian Brethren of Scotland. Sept. 1650.

Jus Patronatus; or, a brief legal **and** rational Plea for Advowsons and **Patrons** ancient, lawful, just, and equitable Rights and Titles **to** present **Incumbents to** Parish Churches **or** Vicaridges upon Vacancies, &c. Lond. **1654. 4to.**

A Declaration **and Protestation against** the Excise. **London. E. Thomas.** 4to. **1654.**

In Works, 1655.

A Seasonable Vindication of the good, **old,** fundamental Liberties of all English Freemen. London. E. Thomas. 4to. 1654.

The First and Second Part of a Seasonable Vindication of the good, old, fundamental Liberties of all English Freemen. **2nd Edition.** London. E. Thomas. 4to. 1655.
   In Works, 1655.
A new Discovery of Free-state Tyranny: containing four Letters; "together with a subsequent Remonstrance of several Grievances and Demands of Common Rights; written and sent by him (Prynne) to Mr. John Bradshaw and his Associates at Whitehall (stiling themselves, The Council of State) after their two years and three months close Imprisonment of him, &c. Lond. 1655. 4to.
A Briefe Polemicall Dissertation concerning the true time of the inchoation and determination of the Lord's-day-Sabbath. London. E. Thomas. 4to. 1655.
   In Works, 1655.
The Quakers unmasked. London. E. Thomas. 4to. 1655.
   In Works, 1655.
A Parliamentary Prognostication made at Westminster for the New-Yeer and Young Members. London. 4to. 1655.
   In Works, 1655.
   1656. Wood, iii. 867.
The Works of William Prynne of Swainswick, Esquire; since his last Imprisonment. London. Edward Thomas. 4to. 1655.
Seasonable Vindication of free Admission to, and frequent Administration of, the holy Communion, to all visible Church Members, regenerate, or unregenerate, &c. Lond. 1656. 4to.
A New Discovery of some Romish Emissaries, Quakers; as likewise of some Popish Errors, unadvisedly embraced, pursued by our Anti-communion Ministers. London. Edward Thomas. 4to. 1656.
Legal Vindication of two important Queries of present general Concernment, clearly discovering from our statute, common, and canon Laws, the bounden Duty of Ministers and Vicars of Parish Churches to administer the Sacraments, as well as preach to their Parishioners, and the legal Remedies against them, in Case of obstinate Refusal. Lond. 1656. 4to.
   Twice printed that year.
   Another title to a copy in Oriel Coll. Wood, iii. 867.

A Short Demurrer to the Jewes long discontinued Remitters into England. London. Edward Thomas. **4to.** 1656.

A Summary Collection of the Principal Fundamental Rights of **all** English Freemen. pp. 32. London. Sm. 4to. 1656.

Another copy of the above; same date, but with considerable additions; pp. 84.

Lord's Supper briefly vindicated, **and clearly demonstrated to** be a **Grace-begetting,** Soul-converting **(not a meer confirming)** Ordinance. **Lond. 1657.**

The Subjection **of all** Traytors, Rebels, as **well** Peers as Commons, **in** Ireland, **to the Laws, Statutes,** and Tryals by Juries of good **and** lawful Men of England, **in the** King's Bench at Westminster, **for** Treasons perpetrated **by them in** Ireland, &c. Being an Argument at Law made in the **Court of** the King's-Bench, Term Hillar. 20 Car. Reg. in the Case of Connor Magwire **an Irish Baron,** &c. Lond. 1658. **4to.**

And 1681.

Probable Expedient for Future **Peace and Settlement.** Lond. 1658.

Twelve serious Queries proposed to all Conscientious Electors of Knights, Citizens, and Burgesses for the Assembly. Lond. 1658.

Twelve several heads **of public** Grievances, and **useful necessary Proposals** of the Western **Counties,** Cities, and Boroughs, to their Knights, Citizens, and Burgesses. 1658.

Eight military Aphorisms, demonstrating **the** Uselessness, Unprofitableness, Hurtfulness, and prodigal Expensiveness of all standing English **Forts** and Garrisons, **to the People of** England, &c. **Lond. 1658. 4to.**

Thomas Campanella, an Italian Friar and second Machiavel. His advice **to the** King of Spain for attaining the universal Monarchy of the World.

With an admonitorie Preface by *William Prynne* of Lincolnes-Inne. London. Philemon Stephens. 4to. **1659.**

A Gospel Plea (Interwoven with **a Rational** and Legal) for the Lawfulness **and** Continuance of **the Antient** settled Maintenance and

APPENDIX.

Tithes of the Ministers of the Gospel. In two parts. The title-page wanting to the first. London. 4to. 1659.
<small>Printed in 1653. Wood, iii. 866.
Reprinted with the second part thereof 1659. Wood, iii. 866.
There is also a book called "The Remainder of the Gospel Plea," &c. Wood, iii. 870.</small>

A Brief Register of the Several Kinds of Parliamentary Writs, in four parts. 4 vols. bound in three. London. 4to. 1659, 1660, 1662, 1664.

Beheaded Dr. John Hewyt's Ghost, pleading, yea crying for exemplary Justice against the misnamed High Court of Justice. Lond. 1659. 4to.
<small>In Oriel Coll. another copy, 1660. Wood, iii. 869.</small>

The true good old Cause rightly stated, and the false uncased. Lond. 1659. 4to.

The Republicans and others spurious good old Cause, briefly and truly anatomized, to preserve our Native Country, Kingdom, legal Government, &c. Lond. 1659. 4to.

New Cheater's Forgeries detected, disclaimed, &c. Lond. 1659.

A True Narrative of what was done by Mr. Prynne and others in the Commons Lobby on the 7th and 9th of this instant May. 4to. 1659.

Ten Considerable Quæries concerning Tithes. London. Edward Thomas. 4to. 1659

Answer to a Proposition, in Order to the Proposing of a Commonwealth or Democracy. Lond. 1659.

Concordia discors: or, the dissonant Harmony of sacred public Oaths, Protestations, Leagues, Covenants, Ingagements, lately taken by many time-serving Saints, Officers, without Scruple of Conscience, making a very unpleasant Consort in the Ears of our most faithful, &c. Lond. 1659. 4to.

A brief necessary Vindication of the old and new secluded Members, from the false malicious Calumnies; and of the fundamental Rights, Liberties, Privileges, &c. from the late avowed Subversions. 1. Of Joh. Rogers in his Christian Concertation with Mr. Will.

Prynne and others. 2. Of March. Nedham in his Interest will not lie, &c. Lond. 1659. 4to.

Short, legal, medicinal, useful, safe, **easy** Prescription to recover **our** Kingdom, Church, Nation, from their present dangerous distractive, **destructive Confusion,** and worse than Bedlam Madness, &c. Lond. 1659. 4to.

Remonstrance of the Noblemen, Knights, Gentlemen, Clergy-men, Free-holders, Citizens, Burgesses, and Commons, of the late Eastern, Southern, Western Association, who desire **to shew themselves faithful and constant to the** good old Cause, &c. Lond. 1659.

Ten Queries upon **the ten new Commandments of** the General Council of the **Officers of the Army, 22 Dec. 1659. 4to.**

Six important **Queries proposed to** the Re-sitting **Rump of the Long** Parliament, fit to be satisfactorily resolved, &c. **Dec. 1659.**

The Privileges of Parliament, which the Members, **Army, and this Kingdom have taken the** Protestation and Covenant to maintain. Reprinted **in 5 Jan. 1659. 4to.**

Conscientious, **serious, Theological, and Legal Queries** propounded to the twice **dissipated, self-created Anti-parliamentary** Westminster Juncto, **and its Members. To convince them of, humble them for,** &c. Lond. **1660. 4to.**

_{Printed in November, 1659. Wood, iii. 870.}

Seven additional Queries in **Behalf of the** secluded Members, propounded to the **twice** broken **Rump now sitting,** the cities of Westminster, **London, &c.** Lond. **1660. 4to.**

_{Published in December, 1659. Wood, iii. 870.}

Case **of the old** secured, secluded, and twice excluded Members, briefly **and truly** stated, for their own Vindication, &c. Lond. 1660. **4to.**

_{Published in December, 1659. Wood, iii. 870.}

Full Declaration of **the true** State of the secluded Members case, in Vindication of themselves and their Privileges, **and of** the respective Counties, &c. Lond. **1660. 4to.**

_{Published in January, 1659.} *

_{* ? 16$\frac{59}{60}$}

Brief Narrative of the Manner how divers Members of the House of Commons, that were illegally and unjustly imprisoned or secluded by the Army's Force in Dec. 1648, and May 7, An. 1659, coming on the 27th of Dec. 1659, to discharge their Trust, were again shut out by the pretended Order of the Members sitting, &c. Lond. 1660. 4to.
: Published latter end December, 1659. Wood, iii. 871.

Copy of the Presentment and Indictment found and exhibited by the Grand Jury of Middlesex on the last day of Hilary Term 1659, against Coll. Matthew Alured, Coll. John Okey, and Others for assaulting and keeping Sir Gilb. Gerard (and other Members) by Force of Arms out of the Commons House of Parl. on 27 Dec. 1659. Lond. 1660.

Three seasonable Queries proposed to all those Cities, Counties, and Boroughs, whose respective Citizens, &c. have been forcibly excluded, unjustly ejected and disabled to sit in the Commons H. by those now acting at Westm. Lond. 1660.
: Published latter end December, 1659. Wood, iii. 871.

Humble Petition and Address of the Sea-men and Water-men in and about the City of Lond. to the L. Mayor, Aldermen and Commons of the City of Lond. in Com. Council assembled, for a free and legal Parliament, &c. Lond. 1660.

Seasonable and healing Instructions, humbly tendered to the Freeholders, Citizens and Burgesses of England and Wales, to be seriously commended by them to their respective Knights, Citizens, Burgesses, elected and to be elected for the next Parliament. 25 Apr. 1660.

Bathonia rediviva. The humble Address of the Mayor, Aldermen, and Citizens of the City of Bath to the King's most excellent Majesty, presented by Mr. Prynne 16 June 1660. Lond. 1660.

The Signal Loyalty and Devotion of God's true Saints and Pious Christians towards their Kings. London. T. C. & L. P. 4to. 1660.
: This was published in two parts; both in the year 1660. See Wood.

A Seasonable Vindication of the Supream Authority and Jurisdiction of

Christian Kings, Lords, Parliaments, as well over the Possessions, as Persons of Delinquents Prelates and Churchmen. **London.** T. Childe & L. Parry. 4to. 1660.

A Supplemental Appendix to the promis'd Disputation of Joh. **Hus.** 1660.

> See **Wood**, iii. 872.

Sundry Reasons humbly tendered to the most honourable House of Peers, **by** some Citizens and Members of **Lond.** and other Cities, Boroughs, Corporations **and** Ports against the new intended Bill for governing and reforming Corporations. 1660.

> Some few of these Reasons were published and the rest suppressed. **Wood,** iii. 872. See Wood.

A Short Sober Pacific Examination of some Exuberances in, and **Ceremonial** Appurtenances to the Common Prayer. London. **T. C. & L. P. 4to.** 1661.

Brevia Parliamentaria Rediviva. In XIII. Sections. **Lond. 4to.** 1662.

> A large-paper copy, stamped on the side with the Royal Arms. Qy. Of Charles II. Qy. If this volume a portion of the Register of Parl. Writs.

Apology for tender Consciences, touching not bowing at the Name of Jesus. Lond. **1662.** 4to.

Aurum Reginæ. London. Thomas Ratcliffe. **4to. 1668.**

The second Tome **of an exact** Chronological Vindication, &c. from **the** first Year **of** K. John 1199, **to** the Death **of K.** Hen. **3.** Dom. 1273, &c. Lond. 1665. Fol.

> Second tome came out before the first. **Wood, iii. 873.**

The first Tome : or, an exact chronological Vindication and historical Demonstration of our British, Roman, Saxon, Danish, Norman, English Kings supreme Ecclesiastical Jurisdiction, in, over all spiritual **or** religious Affairs, Causes, Persons, &c. within **their** Realms **of** England, Scotland, Ireland, and other Dominions, from the original Planting of Christian Religion, **&c. to** the Death of King Rich. I. An. 1199. **Lond.** 1666. **Fol.**

Brief Animadversions on the **Fourth Part of the** Institutes **of the** Laws **of England** compiled by Sir **Edward Cooke.** Lond. **Fol.** 1669.

The History of **King** John, King **Henry III.** and King Edward I. wherein the Sovereign Dominion **of the** Kings of **England over all persons in all causes** is asserted. **Lond.** Fol. 1670.

An **Exact Abridgement** of the Records **in** the Tower of **London.** Collected by Sir Robert Cotton. **London.** Fol. 1689.

    The Preface **is** dated 1656-7.

    The title-page alone appears to be of the date of 1689.

INDEX.

Actresses, Prynne's charge against, 10
Actresses, French, at Blackfriars, 10
Antoninus. *See* **Caracalla**
Arundel, Earl of, his sentence on Prynne, 25
Atkins, alderman of Norwich, 73

Bastwick, John, allowed to go abroad to confer with his counsel, 61; committed to Launceston Castle, 63; removal of, to the Scilly Isles, 64, 68; not to be visited by his wife, 65; notice of his sentence, 75; stands in the pillory, 86; Bible allowed to Prynne, Bastwick, and Burton, 62
Blackfriars, French actresses at, 10
Bodin, quoted against stage plays, 7
Buckner, licenses Histriomastix, 2, 14; his defence, 15; sentences on, 17, 28
Burton, Henry, allowed to go abroad to advise with his counsel, 61; committed to Lancaster Castle, 63; removal of, to Guernsey, 64; not to be visited by his wife, 65, 68; to be carried by sea, 67; notice of his

Burton—*continued*.
  sentence, 75; stands in the pillory, 86

Caligula, his **murder** referred to, 13
Caracalla, Antoninus, story told of, 12
Carlisle, Earl of, his sentence on Prynne, 24
Carnarvon Castle, Prynne's committal to, 62
Carr, Lady Ann, marries Lord Russell, 95
Catlin, his charge against Monson, 92
Charles I., allusions to by Prynne, 10; said to be compared by him to Nero, 11
Charles **VI., King of** France, **accident to,** referred **to by Prynne,** 8
Coke, Sir John, his sentence on Prynne, 22
Commissions against abuse of innkeepers, 76; against excessive brokage, and erecting cottages, 77
Commodus, **his murder** referred to, 13
Common Prayer Book allowed to Prynne, Bastwick, and Burton, 62
Concourse **of** people to Prynne, Bastwick, and Burton, 66
Coryton, sub-warden of the Stanneries, 81

Cottington, **Lord,** his sentence, 16
Crosby, Sir Piers, Wentworth's charge against, 83

Dancing, opinion **of** Prynne on, 4, 11
Dorset, Earl of, his sentence on Prynne, **24**

Edmondes, Sir Thomas, his sentence on Prynne, 23
Elector Palatine, the (Charles Lewis), his proposed return to the Continent, 74
Elizabeth, Queen, suppression of plays by, 5
Essex forest, compositions for lands in, 74
Exeter, Earl of, his sentence on Prynne, 24

Fathers of the **Church** quoted against **stage** plays, 6
Female actors. *See* Actresses
Female **dress, Prynne's** opinion on men wearing, 3; its immodesty complained of by Prynne, 4
Finch, Sir John, charges Prynne with attacking the Queen, 10; suggests that the Queen is intended by Herodias, 11

Fishery, recommended by Laud to the Londoners, 71
France, alleged **alliance** of England **with, 74**; progress of **its army in** the **Spanish Netherlands, 86**

Gallienus, **his** murder referred to, 13
Goad, Dr., consulted by Prynne, 2; his evidence read, 3
Gouge, Dr. murder **of** his son, 81
Guernsey, Burton's removal to, 64

Hamilton, Marquis of, his sentence on Prynne, 25
Harris, Dr., consulted by Prynne, 2; his evidence read, 3
Heliogabalus, example of his acting refered to, 9
Henrietta Maria, alleged attack upon by Prynne, 10
Herodias, her name said **to** have been used to cover Prynne's attack upon the Queen, 11
Histriomastix, Noy's complaint of, **1**; its gradual enlargement, 2

Inn-keepers, abuses of, 76

Jermyn, Sir Thomas, his sentence on Prynne, 22
Jersey, Prynne's removal to, 64
Juxon, Bishop, his sentence on Prynne, 24; abstains from delivering a sentence on Prynne, Burton, and Bastwick, 75

Kilvert, Richard, **his** charges against **Williams,** 89
Kings, their connection with the theatre blamed, 8; their murders related, 13
King's Bench, dispute of with the Stannery Court, 81

Laud, Archbishop, his sentence on Prynne, 26; Prynne's expostulatory letter to, 32; an alderman's answer to, 71; his speech at the sentence of Prynne, Burton, and Bastwick, 75, 83; replies to the Bishop of Lincoln's *Holy Table,* 76; his speech at the censure of Williams, 94
Lincoln, Bishop of. *See* Williams, Bishop
Londonderry, the City fine about, 70, 77

Manchester, Earl of, **his** sentence on Prynne, **25**
Mariana, quoted against stage-plays, 7, 12
Mathews, A., gives **evi**dence that he had printed part of Histriomastix, 3
Maynard, Sir J., his fight with Lord Powis, 80
Mohun, Lord, imprisoned and released, 70; his son sent to the Fleet, 91
Monson, Sir John, Catlin's charge against, 92
Mountnorris, Lord, kisses the King's hands, 83

Neile, Archbishop, his sentence on Prynne, 25

Nero, **his murder referred** to, 13
Newburgh, Lord, his sentence **on** Prynne, 24
Noy, Sir William (Attorney-General), his information against Prynne, 1; his opinion of stage-plays, 2; declares that Prynne had attacked the King, 11

Oxford, University of, its sentence on Prynne, 30

Peacham, **Cottington's** reference **to, 17**
Pembroke, **Earl** of, his sentence on Buckner, 25
Portland, Earl of, his sentence on Prynne, 28
Powis, Lord, his fight with Sir J. Maynard, 80
Prynne, William, the Attorney General's charge against, 1; consults Dr. Goad and Dr. Harris about the publication of Histriomastix, 2; his opinion on female dress **and** dancing, 4; his opinion on play-houses, 5; his alleged attack upon the King, 8; and upon the Queen, 10; his charge against actresses, 10; he is said to have compared the King to Nero, 12; defence of, 14; sentences on, 16-28; his petition to the Privy Council, 29; sentence of the University of Oxford on, 30; his expostulatory letter to Laud, 32; his Histriomastix called in, 58; allowed to go abroad to confer with his counsel, 61; committed to Car-

INDEX. 121

Prynne—*continued.*
narvon Castle, 62; removal of, to Jersey, 64; notice of his second sentence, 75; stands **in** the pillory, 86; **his** verses on his branding, 90; his will, 96; list of his works, 101

Queen. *See* **Henrietta Maria**

Richardson, Chief Justice, his sentence, 20
Russell, Lord, marries Lady Ann Carr, 95

St. Gregory's, its destruction ordered, 72
St. John, Oliver, his papers seized, 77; suspected of framing Burton's answer, 83

Saye **and** Sele, Viscount, his case of ship money, 83
Scilly Isles, Bastwick's removal to, 64
Sparkes, M., Histriomastix shown to, 3, 14; **sentences** on, 17-28
Stage-plays, Noy's opinion of, 2; Prynne's opinion of, 5
Stanhope Lord, resigns the Postmastership, 88
Stannery Court, its dispute with the King's Bench, 81
Star Chamber, **cases in,** against Prynne, **1;** Lord Mohun, **70;** Strangways, Dives, **and** Stradling, 72, 78; **the** Bishop of Lincoln, **73,** 78; Prynne, Burton, and Bastwick, 75; its sentence against the latter drawn up, 91
Suffolk, Earl of, his **sentence** on Prynne, 25

University of Oxford, its sentence on Prynne, 30

Vane, Sir Henry, his sentence on Prynne, 23

Wentworth, Viscount, his charge against Mountnorris, 2; against Crosby, 83
Williams, John, Bishop of Lincoln, proceedings against in the Star Chamber, 73, 78, 84, 85, 88, 91; his *Holy Table, Name, and Thing,* replied **to** by Laud, 76; his sentence in the Star Chamber, 94
Wimbledon, Earl **of, his** sentence on Prynne, **24**

www.ingramcontent.com/pod-product-compliance
Lightning Source LLC
Chambersburg PA
CBHW030243170426
43202CB00009B/605